INSIGHTFUL SELLING

LEARN THE S.A.L.E.S. FORMULA™ TO DIFFERENTIATE
YOURSELF AND CREATE CUSTOMER VALUE

ADON T. RIGG, CME, CSE

Insightful Selling © 2011 Adon T. Rigg, CME, CSE

ISBN-13: 978-1466428607
ISBN-10: 1466428600

Printed in the United States of America
11 12 13 14   5 4 3 2 1

TABLE OF CONTENTS

Chapter 9

The Expose Step - Expose the Problem

SEVEN FACTORS THAT ARE IMPACTING THE TRADITIONAL ROLE OF THE SALES PROFESSIONAL

1. Introduction

I never intended to be in sales. In fact, I dropped out of school to work in the family business – that is, whenever I decided to show up. My father would take me on business meetings where I was exposed to high-level executives in organizations like the Vancouver Canucks. I drove around in a 1979 burgundy Corvette and never paid a bill. My life was great and I had zero responsibility.

That all changed when I was 18 and my family went bankrupt. We moved out of town, and soon after, my parents divorced. Within a matter of a day, I found myself sleeping on a friend's couch with no money, no education, no job skills, and no life skills.

But I had a plan.

Across the street from my friend's place was the welfare office. I made an appointment to get assistance, but when I met with the welfare office I was notified that I was too young; you had to be at least 19 years old to qualify.

Plan B was to get a high-paying job, and I began my search in the local paper. There was an advertisement for a position that started at $20 per hour. I made the call and scheduled a time for my job interview. Once the interview concluded, I was hired as a vacuum cleaner salesperson, a straight commission position demanding 12 hours a day.

I was very successful selling vacuums, but within a few months the company closed. I skated from job to job thereafter. I spent time washing dishes in the morning and worked as a cashier in the evening. For a time I worked as a laborer building log homes, and even spent time as a junior accountant.

I was at home one evening, flicking through the channels, and I noticed a guy from the 80's television show, "That's Incredible!" which had long been canceled. The interviewer was Fran Tarkenton, the famous football player. He was interviewing Anthony Robbins, and I listened for a few minutes, wishing I could afford his personal power audio cassette series. I could barely afford to eat, let alone purchase the tapes: however, by chance shortly after, I found myself in a bookstore in front of his book, "Unlimited Power." I purchased the book and my life has never been the same.

I eventually got my GED and took classes in marketing and sales. I read every book I could find in the realm of self-improvement, business, and sales. I became obsessed with being better, challenging myself to overcome all anxieties and obstacles that were barriers to my advancement.

The next great learning experience in my life was when I read "Maximum Achievement" by Brian Tracy, and I realized that there were universal laws like the law of attraction, law of correspondence, law of super conscious activity, law of cause and effect, law of compensation, law of control, law of concentration and – my personal favorite – the law of belief. Once I began to understand these laws and invested in myself, I grew in confidence and my sales career followed. I was becoming more successful in my approach.

I would again take my sales career to another level when I was introduced to "Spin Selling" by Neil Rackham. The book is based on research of 35,000 sales calls. The research proved what I had intuitively known all along: that closing practices in large sales accounts do not work, and that the most successful salespeople use questioning skills in a specific sequence which he calls "spin" (situation, problem, implication, need payoff).

The culmination of the lessons learned from "Unlimited Power," "Maximum Achievement," and Spin Selling" provided me with the tools to excel in my profession. The more I excelled, the more fun and confidence I obtained. I went on to work for two Fortune 500 companies in executive roles, which included winning the North American Sales Professional of the Year award.

One lesson I have learned and know to be true is that change is constant. What works today may not work tomorrow. So it is in selling. To sell successfully you must change, because what worked yesterday does not work today. That's why I wrote this book. As author of "Selling Change," Brett Clay says, "Change happens. Be the agent."

This book is about making the transition from a salesperson to an *insightful executive*. A traditional salesperson is one who sells a tangible product or service that fills a need. It might be that he or she sells vacuums, safety supplies, filtration systems, or cleaning services. In contrast, an insightful executive is someone who thinks about his offering as an *intangible* regardless of what he sells. That intangible always impacts the profit and loss statements, which is every buyer's responsibility whether he sits in the C-suite or is a junior level purchaser.

The seven game changers addressed in this book have affected the marketplace and are projected to further impact the selling profession. Many business professionals are predicting that of the 18 million salespeople in America, 15 million positions will be eliminated by the year 2020 – an 83% reduction.

Sales professionals who wish to survive must change, or they will become obsolete and irrelevant. Many salespeople today find it challenging to create real value for their customers and are relegated to what I term "order takers." Sellers today must be able to create opportunities and value for today's busy and sophisticated buyers. That is what will separate the traditional sales professional from the insightful executive of the future.

In this book you will be introduced to the S.A.L.E.S Formula™, an acronym-based selling process that will help you to think like an executive who provides insight to his or her customers. Executive insight is what a buyer desires, because it creates value. And value creation is what successful selling in the 21st century requires. In fact, it is the differentiator among competitive businesses and is essential for selling in a crowded and globalized market.

2.   The S.A.L.E.S Formula™

If you want to achieve success, follow the formula.

Often, we think of a "formula" as being interchangeable with "methods" or "processes." But there's a subtle, yet important difference. According to dictionary.com, a "method" is a procedure, technique, or way of doing something. A "process" is a systematic series of actions directed to some end. A "formula," though, is a set form of words, as for stating or declaring something definitely or authoritatively.

As an example, the first time I tried algebra I jumped right in trying to solve problems without reading the textbook. I literally got a headache, and became extremely confused and frustrated – so much so, I had to step away from it for a while. When I later came back to the assignment and followed the directions in the textbook, I learned the formula necessary to solve the equation. That formula was BEDMAS (brackets, exponents, division, multiplication, addition, subtraction). Once I followed this formula, I began solving the equations faster and more successfully. If I didn't follow the formula and tried taking a shortcut, I did not get the solutions I desired, and frustration and failure were the only results.A formula requires specific steps in order to solve an equation. "Process" or "method" can also get you to your destination; however, the results are not as measurable. The S.A.L.E.S Formula™ requires the sales professional to follow each step in the specific order to be successful. As with algebra, it takes time to learn the formula and to become comfortable with it, but once the formula has been mastered, solving the equation becomes easier.

Think of the S.A.L.E.S Formula™ as a guide that will position you as an insightful executive who sits in the boardroom of your company. The S.A.L.E.S Formula™ will empower you with the confidence necessary to influence those in any suite including the C-suite.

There are many great sales books available, but this book provides you with the additional powerful methods of the S.A.L.E.S Formula™. It is broken down as follows:

Study – Do your research before you make your sales call, because success is all about pre-call planning, positioning, and prospecting. These skills contribute to over 70% of your success, even before you've had your first meeting.

Ask – The go ASK process will ensure that you're asking questions created around a hypothesis to provoke, inspire, and motivate the buyer to desire change.

Learn – How you can impact the buyer's bottom line, which always aligns with his or her organizational goals and operational processes.

Expose – Reveal the implications or consequences of the buyer's current condition through your questioning process. Challenge the status quo.

Solve - Once the buyer recognizes a problem, present your solution using your product or service. The S.A.L.E.S Formula™ doesn't close customers. It opens relationships.

It is important to remember that the S.A.L.E.S Formula™ is dependent upon your following and completing each step before you proceed to the next, while ensuring your prospect is on the same step with you.

Ask yourself this important question: What do you want for your future? A huge shift in the sales world is coming, and many sales professionals will find their jobs disappearing. The remainder of this book will provide you with the tools to set yourself apart, differentiate your executive skills, and place you alongside any executive in the boardroom.

CHAPTER 1
– Selling Is about Creating Change

A New Frontier

It's a new world out there.
The world of sales has changed dramatically over the last decade, and it will continue to change over the next. The terms "salesman," "salesperson," and "sales professional" mean something different in this brave new world; surviving in the world of sales means changing with the times.

Selling, as We Know it, Is Dead.

In the next ten years, there will be a massive paradigm shift in the relevance and contribution of a company's sales force. The traditional "salesperson" will be gone, and a new breed of sales professional will lead companies to success.

This new sales professional won't rely on tricks and techniques to make sales. This sales professional will rely on the personal – understanding of a customer's challenges and needs, building collaborative relationships with every new business contact from the junior-level position to the C-suite, and mastering the art of good communication – in order to succeed.

It is important to understand the seven game changers and the four attributes that are impacting and changing today's sales force. This will allow the sales professional to make the transition to what I term an "insightful executive" who sits alongside C-level executives in the boardroom. The S.A.L.E.S Formula™ will transform your sales career by setting you apart from the competition. Changing the way you think about sales while opening the door to a successful sales future.

Before we discuss how the sales profession is being redefined today, let's take a look at how the profession has evolved and how it's changed over the last few decades.

For clarification purposes only, let's define a salesperson as one earning his or her income from selling goods or services. (This certainly includes entrepreneurs and small business owners.)

Industrial Revolution

The sales profession began to take shape during the industrial revolution of the 18th century. In the latter part of the 18th century, the British economy began to shift from a manual labor and draft animal-based economy to a machine-based manufacturing economy. As goods became easier to manufacture and ship, international trade expanded and the cost of production dropped. Demand for these goods and services increased, and this increased demand from new markets dictated a new class of professional dedicated to his sale.

These new professionals traveled with their products and introduced them to the new and expanding market of potential customers. This means of selling goods – the "sales call" – was highly effective and a powerful way to introduce goods to consumers. This was the beginning of the traveling sales person; this profession was key in expanding distribution and ensuring the movement of products throughout the world.

Post Industrial Revolution

By the late part of the century, the sales profession was part of everyday life, but it was changing, evolving into a profession with defined skills, tactics, rules and expectations. The sales person was transformed from a simple seller of goods to the professional salesperson

armed with a polished script. This transformation pushed the profession forward, but it also contributed to the negative portrayal of the profession.

Charles W. Hoyt chronicled this transition in 1912, showing two types of salespeople.

"The old kind of salesman is the "big me" species.... He works for himself and, so far as possible, according to his own ideas.... There is another type of salesman. He is the new kind. At present he is in the minority, but he works for the fastest growing and most successful houses of the day. He works for the house, and the house works for him. He welcomes and uses every bit of help the house sends to him." [1]

The Two World Wars and the Depression

The sales profession faced obstacles during the two World Wars and through the Depression. The financial hardship caused by two global wars and a severe economic depression made it near impossible for any but the strongest businesses to survive. This severe economic environment helped an aggressive style of selling to grow and flourish.

Once the country moved past this time of economic peril, strong salespeople were considered important contributors to the survival of their organizations. Salespeople were seen as critical players in a business's success, and they were respected for their abilities to drive revenue growth.

Post World War II

In the 1950s customers became less tolerant of the high-pressure, manipulative sales approach that had prospered in the war years. So selling changed with the times, becoming less aggressive and more professional. Since then the professional salesperson has become an integral part of a company's growth. The role has expanded from simply a presenter of information to one that encompasses a variety of responsibilities, including training customers and assisting in the management of projects alongside them.

But change is inevitable. And as the world evolves in this new information and technological age, the role of the sales professional is in the process of redefining itself once again.

Why Sales People Were Necessary

More money is spent on personal selling than on any other form of marketing communications, including advertising, sales promotion, publicity, and public relations. [2]

It's important to look at the traditional role and function of the salesperson in the business world as it relates to the medium of advertising.

In the past, the sales team and their ability to generate sales growth shouldered the responsibility for relaying a company's message, because direct sales was cheaper and more effective than other methods. Before our current information and technology age, the sales force could send the message directly to the decision maker and close the sale in the most cost effective manner (usually commission). The cost could easily be measured by cost per rep vs. sales generated, and it was considered the greatest return on investment (ROI).

Personal selling cost more in pennies per customer in comparison to television and radio advertising. But from a B2B (business to business) perspective, more time and money would be wasted advertising on television and other outlets if you desired to target specific markets. A strong and effective sales team could identify, target, and close a sale in a much more timely fashion.

A relationship was created between the seller and the buyer, and this could only be accomplished with physical contact in the form of a sales call. At the time this was the only way that people could meet and create relationships. Most people met and married someone from the same school, church, or community because people had smaller and more confined spheres of reference. This kind of personal interaction established trust, which in turn built relationships. The world has changed dramatically over the last decade, and the dependence on salespeople to provide information has been affected by seven game-changing events.

The Seven Game Changers

The Internet

The Internet has changed the world, and in changing the world, it's forever changed the way business is conducted. The Internet has changed the way we apply and look for work. It's revolutionized the way we look for companionship. It's transformed the way we buy concert tickets and books, or confirm hotel reservations, cars, and airfares. It's changed the way people learn, and it's irrevocably changed us.

We will, no doubt, continue to see the growing power and influence of the Internet as it affects many of the things we take for granted: the daily newspaper, movies, music, home telephones, mail delivery, and traditional banking. We will also see the Internet change the way the educational system teaches our young people. Already 80% of Canadians have a high speed Internet connection, and other countries are fast approaching this statistic. Young people today don't remember a world without text messaging or the Internet, and many of us are connected to friends, family, and business associates 24/7/365.

The Internet has turned a very specialized and localized global community into an intimate, interconnected community where everything is just a click away. How different is this new world? Consider this: Can you imagine spending $3000 on a set of encyclopedias?

Best Practices

Another game changer for today's sales professional is the sophistication of business operations and practices. In the past, a company that offered on-time delivery, guaranteed stock, or value-added tools had a real competitive advantage over other companies incapable of offering the same thing. A company's sales team could leverage these best practices, and customers considered them real incentives to do business with their companies.

Today, it's a different ball game. On-time delivery, guaranteed stock, and value-added tools are available from any company, and the customer no longer considers these a benefit. Today, these best practices are an expected part of the customers' experience, and they consider it a natural part of the purchasing process.

Many purchasers and decision makers are encouraged to use operational excellence to maximize efficiencies, reduce costs, and trim reliance on suppliers. Through the use of management strategies like Six Sigma, companies are limiting the number of vendors they use in an effort to maximize rebates and discounts, strengthen purchasing power, and reduce costs within their supply chain. Many companies use practices such as just-in-time inventory, established standard operating procedures, and integrated systems with their suppliers. In many cases, these practices create a strong interdependence between the companies involved, and the cost of change comes at a higher risk to the decision maker.

There's also an increasing pressure for companies to comply with regulatory demands such as non-discriminatory practices, accounting compliance, and occupational health and safety compliance. In these cases, not only does switching suppliers come at a higher cost, it also forces companies to deal with potential regulatory issues as well.

To illustrate the potential for personal accountability within an organization, consider the Canadian bill C-45 (the summary that follows comes directly from http://www.cca-acc.com/news/government/billc45/summary.pdf):

"The Criminal Code amendments outlined in Bill C-45 are in part a response to the findings of the Westray mining disaster public inquiry. On May 9, 1992, 26 miners died after an explosion at the Westray coal mine in Plymouth, Nova Scotia. A subsequent inquiry laid blame on Westray management and two provincial government departments.

The Westray experience brought attention to the current difficulty in finding criminal liability on the part of corporations, (see explanation below). It also contributed to a perceived need for a clear statement in the Criminal Code that wanton or reckless disregard for the safety of workers and the public at large in a workplace setting is a criminal offence.

Bill C-45 introduces amendments to the Criminal Code that amend the definition of "everyone" and "person" to include "an organization". It also establishes rules for attributing criminal liability to organizations, including corporations, for the acts of their representatives and also creates a legal duty for all persons directing work to take "reasonable steps" to ensure the safety of workers and the public."

Commoditization

In today's economy, sales professionals face a daunting challenge: competition isn't simply the next salesman at the competing company. Competition is everywhere, and it's only a click away.

Sophisticated business practices, innovative technology, and the Internet have made product differentiation almost nonexistent; it's not uncommon for a sales professional to spend considerable time and effort creating interest and providing a quote only to lose the sale or sell at a much lower margin. Today, customers simply go online and use search engines like Google and Yahoo! to find comparable products at a lower price point.

With the ability to compare prices in a matter of moments, sales professionals often find themselves educating a potential customer on a product's benefits, only to have the customer go online and get a better price from a competitor. This puts the sales representative in a very tough position when obtaining a healthy margin is her mandate. The relationship with the customer can become strained if there is a feeling that the representative has charged too much. But customers might not consider the value of the time and effort spent in educating them and driving the sale.

There was a time when exclusive distribution allowed for a company to avoid this trap. Unfortunately, that world has gone the way of the dinosaurs. As the similarities of competing companies have grown more significant, product differentiation has become marginal. Many companies struggle to increase margin and differentiate their products by establishing a private label line, only to learn that the competition has exactly the same private labeled product from the same supplier! The only difference between them is the company logo and the price the customer pays for it.

The winner is the consumer, who receives a quality product at an excellent price. But this win for consumers comes at the expense of the sales representative's commission and the company's profit margin.

Rising Inflation

Even if companies find a way to face and overcome the challenges of the Internet culture, product differentiation, commoditization, they will find rising costs an important and unavoidable game changer.

Rising costs are a very real contributing factor to the imminent demise of the traditional sales representative. The cost of business is high: expenses like salaries, health benefits, pension plans, medical insurance, heat, electricity, rent, taxes, and gas affect the bottom line in all businesses sectors. Many businesses find themselves relying on yearly price increases to assist them in meeting these rising expenses. This only exacerbates the problem.

As the costs of running a business skyrocket, businesses are forced to make tough decisions about which expenses are absolutely essential. This challenge, combined with margin compression and limited profitable growth, makes the cost of maintaining a sales force less viable than it once was. It's no longer cost-effective or necessary to make face-to-face sales calls for a customer to place an order.

As sales teams find themselves becoming a non-essential business expense, the nature of the sales professional must change.

Changing Demographics

Another game changer for today's sales professional is the changing demographics of consumers in the marketplace.

The baby boom generation, which makes up approximately one-quarter of the population of Canada and the United States (84.5 million people), has long been the central demographic of consumers. Many of the roots of traditional sales philosophies reflect the needs and consumption patterns of the baby boom generation. This generation grew up in the old world with parents affected by the wars and the Great Depression. Baby boomers saw technology change slowly (in contrast to the rapid technological shifts of today). The major cultural markers for this generation include purchasing a color television, shifting from AM radio to FM, and watching the strong family unit dissolve into the free love of the Beatles, drugs, and the birth control pill.

But the baby boom generation is starting to retire, and two new generational demographics are moving up to take their place. Generation X and Generation Y, the new younger generations, are rising to prominence and reshaping the consumer world.

Generation X, the generation born between 1964 and 1984, represents approximately 46 million people in North America. This generation saw change at a much faster rate than did their parents, the baby boom generation. In a matter of years, Gen Xers saw video game technology grow from Pong to Atari, from Atari to Intellivision, from Intellivison to Colecovision, and from Colecovision to PlayStation 1. Generation X saw the creation of the VCR, the change from cassette tape to compact disc, the shift from Commodore 64 to the 486 33 MHz processor, the FM radio station giving way to MTV music television and Canada's Much Music, the telephone's evolution to the fax machine and the pager, and the introduction of the bank card. Many Generation Xers are proving more technologically adaptable than were their predecessors:

many have adopted all the technological changes that their children have grown up taking for granted. However, there is a substantial percentage in jeopardy of becoming irrelevant as their children's Generation Y enters the marketplace.

Generation Y, the almost 80 million born between 1984 and 2000, is poised to revolutionize the marketplace. This generation has seen an incredible explosion of technology: from the cellular phone and the Internet to the Internet on their mobile smartphone. This generation created Facebook, YouTube, and Twitter. They only know of a world where connection to their friends and family via the Internet is constant. This generation has seen the changes from dial-up to wireless, from CDs to the iPod, from the cellular phone to the handheld tablet computer, from music stores to iTunes, from MTV to on-demand television, from PlayStation to graphics-rich online gaming, and from the ATM to online. As the baby boom generation rides into the sunset to enjoy a much deserved retirement and Generation X and Generation Y fill their vacant position, massive change is happening to the old way of doing business.

Sales 2.0

Another game changer is sales 2.0 and is best explained by the bestselling book, "Sales 2.0," by authors Anneke Seley and Brent Holloway[3]:

What is sales 2.0? It is the use of innovative sales practices, focused on creating value for both the buyer and seller and enabled by Web 2.0 and next generation technology. Sales 2.0 practices combine the science of process driven operations with the art of collaborative relationships, using the most profitable and most expedient sales resources required to meet customers' needs. This approach produces superior, predictable, repeatable business results, including increased revenue, decreased costs, and sustained competitive advantage. It is the practice of inter-related interdependent categories: strategy, people, process, and technology.

Strategy:
Your most experienced and expensive sales team should be focused on your largest qualified customers or sales opportunities. You can leverage their time and attention with a sales strategy that includes resources dedicated to sales opportunities that don't requires face to face interaction. Sales 2.0 leverages the most expensive sales reps while keeping the sales pipeline consistently full, increasing customer acquisition and revenue generation. This keeps cost of sales low to deliver maximum value to investors and shareholders.[3]

People:
The focus is on building relationships with customers and peers. Open-minded reps use the phone and web extensively in place of on-site visits to contain costs, improve productivity, and provide more immediate service. Team selling goals and individual goals are supported by compensation plans that reward sales 2.0 behavior.[3]

Process:
Sales 2.0 process is designed with customers at the forefront and asks about their business initiatives? What action must they take at each step? What do they need from you and by when? Are you easy to do business with? This customer-focused process gives you a framework by which to measure your business metrics and key performance indicators (KPIs) to figure out what's working and what's not. Without it you can't predict business results.[3]

Technology:
The predictability, constant improvement in business processes, and strong, engaged online relationships that are the hallmark of sales 2.0 are supported by technology. It may be customer relationship management (CRM), business analytics, e-mail, and website tracking software, or products that accelerate account research or lead generation that help make sales reps more effective and efficient. Or it may be video e-mail, webinar software, or sales portals that encourage interaction, collaboration, and engagement. Without today's technology enabling detailed sales process measurement and analysis – as well as the success of meaningfully building relationships without in-person meetings – Sales 2.0 simply wouldn't be possible.[3]

Web 1, 2, and 3.0

Never heard of Web 3.0? Don't worry. You soon will. And it will be one of the most important game changers for sales professionals.

Web 1.0   1994-2001

The span of time from the initial launch of the Internet until 2001 is often referred to as "Web 1.0." There were high hopes for the Internet during this time, with many speculating – rightly – that the Internet would change the world. The change, however, didn't come as quickly as many thought.

Since the expectations of the Internet exceeded the reality of the time – this was the time of a dial-up connection with websites predominantly information-based – the Internet bubble was created. Many speculators lost their money and their businesses during this time of rapid expansion and collapse. But the ones that did survive the bubble, such as Wikipedia and Amazon, continue to provide excellent service and have laid the groundwork for the evolution of online businesses.

Web 2.0   2001 to Present

Shortly after the start of the millennium, the Internet expanded beyond simple information delivery and became easier for the average person to use. Thanks to sites like homestead.com and Wordpress.com, "do-it-yourself" web design became possible, and individuals could set up home bases online without the aid of a web designer. The evolving Web allowed for more collaboration between the consumer and the interface, exemplified by sites like LinkedIn and Facebook.

Prior to this, business promotion was handled first-hand, with associations like the Rotary Club or the Chamber of Commerce. In the Web 2.0 world, self-promotion is merely a click away on the computer, at sites that are available 24 hours a day, 7 days a week, and 365 days a year.

This shift has made networking and using the Internet the preferred method of communication for Generation X and especially for Generation Y. It has replaced the order-taking, information-providing sales rep. Customers no longer need to phone and wait for the sales rep's next visit to obtain information and answer questions. Now, they can simply go online to a company's website and retrieve information, leave an email question, or get live online assistance. The Internet, and more specifically Web 2.0, provides customers a reliable means of obtaining information, and it lets them rectify issues at their convenience, on their time.

Web 2.0 has also changed the way business is performed for many industries. As an example, look at my own company, Insightful Selling Solutions (www.insightfulselling.com). I can log into the back-end of my website to make any changes necessary. I can check orders, note the number of visitors to my site, and much more. I can also visit my customer relationship management program and update customer contact information, manage my email marketing campaign, and link to social networking sites like Twitter, Facebook, and LinkedIn. I can use Google calendaring for time management and appointments. And with the click of a button, I can have my calendar either email or text message me to remind me of my upcoming meetings. I can access my files anytime and anywhere in the world.

Web 2.0 even answers the need for a phone line. For as little as $10 per month with www.my1voice.com, you can receive a 1-800 number which includes as many extensions as you like, and you can have any voice messages emailed or text messaged to you. This service allows you to manage your extensions, voice messages, call forwarding, personal greetings, and other services anytime from any Internet port in the world.

Web 2.0 has made the cost of doing business very affordable and universally available, on demand at your convenience. Should you need to talk to a company's sales 2.0 team, you can either email them, phone them, or instant message them any time of day and have all your questions and concerns addressed immediately. It took time, but now most people are growing more comfortable with this immediate online business world. And now, many can't imagine not having Web 2.0 as part of their daily business operations; they don't know how they got by without it.

Web 3.0

Web 3.0 is still in its infancy, but it's poised and ready to change the world.

Web 3.0 will be the place where people live their lives in both a virtual and a real world. Websites such as SecondLife.com provide this alternative world; sites like it are growing their membership base in record numbers every year. And as social media sites like Facebook and Twitter grow and connect to other businesses, people will do more of their living – and decision-making – through these online mediums.

The potential for this platform is incredible, and many companies are already using these virtual worlds to sell their merchandise, launch new products, and establish collaborative relationships with their customers. The future for Web 3.0 is still in flux, but the possibilities will make it incredibly interesting, indeed.

These are the seven game changers.
1. Internet
2. Best practices
3. Commoditization
4. Rising Inflation
5. Changing demographics
6. Sales 2.0
7. Web 3.0

These seven game changers are major contributors to the demise of the traditional sales representative. The sales professional of tomorrow will not be an individual with a designated territory. He or she won't have the responsibility of a large customer base worth a certain amount of dollars with high autonomy. The future sales professional will not be the cradle-to-grave developer of an account as we know it today. To quote Neil Reckham, author of "Spin Selling": "The world no longer needs a walking, talking brochure."

What the business world needs is a professional individual who understands business. It needs an individual who has excellent relationship skills and presenting skills, and one who is comfortable with technology and change. It needs someone who understands the hidden costs of doing business, understands the industry he or she is in and the industry of the customer. It needs someone who understands the wants, needs, and desires of his or her customers and prospects. And it needs a sales professional who can build collaborative relationships with his own support team, as well as the customer who sits in the C-suite.

"My notion is that selling is dead. These days [salespeople] have to be customer productivity experts,"
Jeff Immelt, CEO, General Electric.[4]

The sales rep of the future is better described as an executive, one who understands how to read a financial statement and how to make a positive impact on his customer's organizational goals and operations. The executive of the future will incorporate and understand the S.A.L.E.S Formula™ and use it in his day-to-day business transactions, making himself an integral part of his company's executive team – someone his company will fight to keep and someone who has an important place in the executive boardroom.

Four Types of Customer Relationships

The first step in transforming yourself from a traditional sales professional to an "executive with insight" is to place a high premium on building effective relationships with your customers.

First, let's consider some important realities. Your customers' needs are important, but it's also important to consider the return on effort (ROE) necessary to provide that service. It is also important to remember the Pareto Principle (better known as "the 80/20 rule") which states that 80 percent of your sales will come from only 20 percent of your customers.

Think about it. You have to work hard to generate successful sales. And realistically, only 20 percent of the relationships you build will generate the overwhelming majority of your sales success. It only makes sense to place relationship-building at a high priority. While it's important to provide excellent service to all customers and to generate new business relationships all the time, it is equally important to ensure that you're concentrating your time on building the right relationships with the right prospects.

To do this effectively it is important to understand the four different types of relationships you'll be creating with any prospective client.

The four different types of relationships are:

1. Transactional relationships
2. Solutions relationships
3. Partnership relationships
4. Collaborative relationships

A transactional relationship is when the buyer and seller interact during a short time-frame in exchange for goods at a given price. This kind of relationship is the most fundamental and most common. Retail outlets and convenience stores have transactional relationships with their customers. The time invested with respect to cost of service is limited and the commitment level to the customer is also limited.

A solutions relationship happens when the cost to service that relationship and the commitment level increases from that of a transactional relationship. In a solutions relationship, the interaction between customer and sales professional includes coaching, teaching, or guidance. Retail outlets like tire stores create this type of relationship with their customers since making a decision on tires can require more time invested on behalf of both parties. A solutions relationship requires more personal investment.

A partnership relationship happens when a company creates a relationship with the customer over an extended period of time. These relationships grow over time, and they become mutually beneficial for both parties. The company invests substantial time to serve the customer by meeting with them regularly and assisting them in improving their position. In return, the customer establishes trust and works with the company to solve their issues.

A collaborative relationship deeply entwines customer and company. In a collaborative relationship, a company works with a client over time to develop a personalized and customized service, one that the client makes integral to his business life. An example of a collaborative relationship would be when a supplier invests a considerable amount of time to create and modify an existing online ordering system to meet the customer's need. The company invests a great deal of time and talent crafting a highly personalized system. The customer, in turn, is tied to the company since the cost of changing suppliers once this program is in place would be exorbitant. These relationships don't work for every customer or company, but they are the deepest and most lasting kind of business relationships.

The chart that follows is from "Sales Management Analysis and Decision Making," 6th edition and illustrates these different relationships and how they relate to commitment and cost.

Relationship Strategies Model

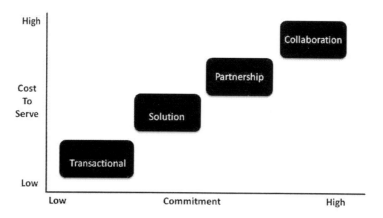

Note that both the cost to serve and the commitment level increases as the relationship progresses from transactional to collaborative. The cost is low to create a transactional relationship, but the rewards aren't as long-lasting. On the other hand, the time necessary to create a collaborative relationship can be high, but the reward is interdependence between the buyer and seller, forming the basis of a long-term relationship.

Return on Time

Lasting relationships are difficult to build with potential and existing customers. They require a lot of time and energy; the smart sales professional will make informed decisions about which relationships to nurture more aggressively.

It's worth taking the time to analyze your existing customer base, looking specifically at what each relationship offers on return on time. This process can assist you in looking at your business with fresh eyes, weighing the time you invest in each customer, his service requirements, and the profit per transaction or per order. Estimate the return on effort and the time you anticipate investing for a specific client relationship. For those relationships you are unsure of, look at other accounts that are similar or in the same industry.

If you're unable to determine the potential for an account and don't have any purchasing history, ask your sales manager for his or her suggestions. If you're an entrepreneur, do an Internet search and look for information that may assist you in making this determination. You can perform this analysis at any time, preferably at least once a year for all existing accounts.

Four Essential Skills to Successful Selling in the 21st Century

Insightful selling is developed through the effective use of four executive skills product knowledge, industry knowledge, executive insight, and questioning skills. In the coming chapters, we will reveal in great detail how to apply the S.A.L.E.S. Formula™, improve your customer's business, and become an executive who sits in the C-suite.

The prerequisite to success is using the information contained within the pages of this book and watching your sales success improve. Let's begin!

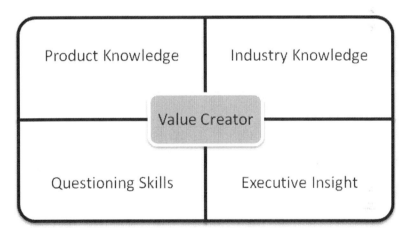

1. Executive Insight: the Language of Business

To walk the walk, you'll need to talk the talk.

To position yourself for success as a sales professional in the 21st Century, you'll need to learn the language of business. Language matters; we trust people who communicate well, and we do business with those we trust.

The language of businesses is financial in nature. Whether you are calling on the CEO or checking in with the purchaser of office supplies.. Different contacts will be interested in different things – the CEO will be interested in all five categories of the income statement and the purchaser will be more focused on the expense section – but the ability to converse in the language of business with both parties make you a more viable sales professional.

Your responsibility as a sales professional is to assist your client or business associate in meeting his or her objectives and to understand where you can make the most substantial impact to his or her business. In order to clearly determine how your product or service can positively impact the customer's profit/loss statement (another word for income statement), it is important to have a fundamental understanding of this very important financial measure.

The Income Statement

There are different descriptions for the income statement, such as profit/loss statement, statement of earnings, or statement of income. But they all refer to the same thing. An income statement is a document which shows the profitability (or loss) of the company for a certain period of time, typically every quarter. It states the revenues earned and expenses incurred during the prescribed time frame.

There are five basic categories on an income statement: revenue, cost of goods, gross profit (or profit margin), expenses, and net profit.

Revenue

Revenues are the total amount earned during a specific time. This could be in product sales, services, and fees. But it could also be concerned with earnings from interest, dividends, leases, or royalties.

Cost of Goods Sold

The cost of goods sold (also "cost of sales" or "cost of service") refers to the total cost of the product before you have sold it. Consider a retail outlet selling shoes. The cost the retailer pays for the shoes to get them into the store is the cost of goods.

Gross Profit

The difference between the selling price and the cost of goods is the gross profit (also profit margin). Consider again a retail shoe store. If the shoe retailer sells the shoes for $30 and bought them for $20, the gross profit would be $10. The profit margin is the same figure, typically expressed as a percentage.

```
Revenue   $30.00
Cogs       $20.00
Profit     $10.00
```

The gross profit is $10. The profit margin 33% (10 /30= .33)

Expenses

Expenses are the costs incurred to generate revenue. These include such things as rent, salaries, utilities, and other business expenses.

Net Profit

The net profit is the total revenue minus both the cost of goods sold and expenses. The net profit is also considered in casual business language as "the bottom line."

Understanding the language of business is an important factor in differentiating and distinguishing yourself as an insightful executive. In an upcoming chapter we will spend a great deal of time examining how you can impact your customer's income statement in a positive and substantial way. For now, it is only important to remember that the language of business is financial, and that the income statement is what your clients and associates are talking about when you hear them say, "It's all about the bottom line."

2. Product knowledge

Here's a simple fact: You can't sell something you don't know.

Product knowledge is important to the sales professional of the 21st century. Without a complete and in-depth knowledge of your product or service, you are at a disadvantage when connecting with customers. Customers equate knowledge with competence, confidence with trustworthiness. If you want to make the sale, know what you're selling. Here are some questions to consider when developing your product knowledge:

What is your product or service?
What does your product offer?
What are the features of your product/service?
What are the advantages of your product/service?

What are the benefits of your product/service?
What is the turnaround time for production?
What similar product like it leads the industry?
How is your product different?
How is your product better?
How is your product priced?
What problems does your product solve?
What payment terms do you accept?
What is your best price?
What is the warranty?
How does the warranty work?
What does your product smell like?
What does your product taste like?
How tall is your product?
Do you have stock?
Is it biodegradable?
How can this product or service impact the customer's income statement?
What does the product weigh?

Some of these questions will be relevant to your product or service, and some will not. But the more you know about your product or service, the more influential you'll be in convincing your clients they can and should do business with you.

Short pencil

A man named John, who was a great influence on my life, used to say, "A short pencil is better than long memory."

I try to remember that. Write down the information about your product and keep it handy. I find that customers don't mind it when I refer to my notes for detailed information. They know you can't remember everything, but if you keep your detailed notes handy and can answer their questions with confidence and completeness it shows you're willing to go the extra mile for them. It reflects positively on you and helps you develop trust with your customer.

3. Industry Knowledge / Credentials

Knowledge in your industry comes from more than just your age or the number of years of experience you have in your industry. It's more than that. Industry knowledge has everything to do with how you've positioned and marketed yourself within your industry, and what you've learned about it. It's about combining what you know about achieving the bottom line with what you know about the product or service you're selling. It's bringing together everything you know and putting it to use.

Your industry knowledge and how you're perceived within your industry is often the starting point for customers when deciding if they need what you offer. The question is always, "Why should I change from the status quo and deal with you and your company?" The answer is in your ability to understand the income statement while using your industry knowledge to make an impact on either the way they generate revenue, the cost of goods, profit margin, expenses, or their bottom line.

Don't Sell Product

It is important to ALWAYS remember that you aren't simply selling a product. You're selling what that product can DO for your customer. Customers don't care about the product you're offering. They can get that product from a variety of sources for a variety of prices. What they care about is the benefit your product or service offers them.

People don't pay a premium price for a BMW just because it starts, has four wheels, and gets them from point A to point B. (If that's all they wanted, they'd buy a $500 automobile from any used car dealer.) What they're buying is the benefits a BMW provides. One customer may purchase it for the smooth drive and comfort. Another might purchase it for the social status she believes the car will give her. In both scenarios they're not buying a motor and four tires. They are satisfying a need by purchasing a solution.

Here's an example of these ideas in action: One of my sales representatives, Ben (not his real name), met with a major BSC (building service contractor) in the janitorial industry who held the contract for a large grocery store retailer. Before the first call, Ben did as much pre-call planning as possible, including visiting the grocery store outlets in the early morning and late evening to determine if the appearance of the store was drastically different at each of these times. He reviewed the quality of the cleaning on the floor, especially in inconspicuous areas. He also did an Internet search on the building service contractor and on the retailer to determine if there were additional opportunities outside of this one outlet location and to obtain any relevant knowledge that might help him for his coming appointment. The final result was that Ben introduced a thicker floor finish along with a tool that allowed the janitors to apply the finish without using a traditional mop and bucket. This accomplished two key benefits for the customer:

- Using a thicker product meant fewer coats were needed. Time needed to apply the finish was reduced.
- Using the new application tool increased the output from 2000 ft² per hour to 4000 ft² per hour.

These two benefits made such a dramatic impact to the building service contractor's income statement that Ben created a customer for life. Using the thicker product meant the time to service the 10,000 square-foot building was reduced by half. This savings added over $40,000 to the company's bottom line. The benefit of this product and the use of the application tool allowed the company to take on additional work. With the hours saved per night, the company made more revenue and increased their employees' income through the company's profit-sharing incentive program.

The income statement was affected in the following ways:

Revenue – This new product allowed the business to take on additional jobs with the time saved, providing an increase in revenue.

Gross profit – This also increased the gross profit of the company, as their costs of goods were not affected, but the margin percentage increased.

Expenses – Expenses were impacted by the huge reduction on labor, on a cost per job perspective.

Net profit – The benefit for everyone in the company was the improved net profit, making the company more viable. This allowed them to allocate additional funds to the marketing and sales division to search for additional jobs and employ more people.

Ben applied his industry knowledge by understanding the language of business and the language of his industry. He was able to leverage his expertise to recommend a product that would create a mutually beneficial relationship. He also positioned himself in the eyes of his customer as a sharp, competent business professional about to positively impact their business.

This was all made possible using the four executive skills necessary for success in the 21st century.

4. Questioning Skills

Want the answer to success? Ask the right questions.

Good questioning skills are an essential component of a sales professional's success. They help you learn more about the organizational processes of the client company so you can positively impact their income statement. Good questioning skills also help the sales professional achieve one or both of the following objectives:

a. Improve a current problem the clients company is experiencing or assist them with uncovering an unseen problem.

b. Discover what goals and objectives the company and/or their specific department have for that particular year or quarter.

It is essential to position yourself as someone who can positively impact your client's business. Asking the right questions will not only afford you the information you need to close the sale, but it will also allow your customer to see your executive knowledge and expertise.

We will explore the fundamentals of good questioning skills in more detail in another section of this book.

Open-ended Questions

Who, what, when, where, why, and how questions are called open-ended questions. They encourage the customer to provide a detailed, thought-provoking response. You want to avoid asking closed questions, which promote a simple yes or no answer. A stronger emphasis on asking open-ended questions will allow you to obtain useful detail and greater insight into the operations and goals of the company.

Here are some strong open-ended questions to consider:

1. What do you like about your current supplier?
2. What would solving this issue mean to your department?
3. How much support for improving this issue do you have from your managers?
4. What does your current supplier do exceptionally well?
5. On a scale of 1 to 10, how would you rate your satisfaction level on the following…?
6. What are the biggest issues you've faced in the last 12 months?
7. How have these issues affected revenue?
8. When would you like this issue resolved?
9. What do you mean by that?
10. How do you mean exactly?

CHAPTER 2 - *The Study Step (Part 1)*
Positioning

Studying and gathering information about your prospect before your first meeting will place you in a position to make the greatest impact on them. The first step in the S.A.L.E.S. Formula™ solution is to position yourself as a professional who can make an impact on your prospect's business. You need to create an impression in the mind of the buyer that you are someone she prefers to do business with.

Perception is reality, and the perception that the buyer has of you is her reality. Everything you do or say positions you in either a positive or negative light; the higher you are positioned in the buyer's mind, the greater your likelihood of success. One of the three essential steps in the study phase is to position yourself in the buyer's mind; this is done by creating your personal brand.

Branding

What is branding? It's all about associations.

If you were to ask ten people to define "branding," you would probably receive ten different answers. The most common answer is that branding is their logo, their company's familiar saying, the promise their company makes, or their catchy tag line. These answers are not incorrect; they're just not the whole story.

Branding is all about association. Branding is the cumulative effect of the associations your customer makes with your product, service, or company – even when the associations aren't necessarily the truth. The feelings, beliefs, emotions, and reactions one has when they hear, see, smell, touch, or taste anything related to your company are the associations that make up your company's brand. So it's vital to think about and see your company from every possible angle.

When you hear the word Starbucks, what immediately comes to your mind? Do you have positive associations with the company's drinks? Do you have negative associations with service you received? Are you just indifferent because you haven't experienced the brand? Those associations count. When you think of McDonald's, what mainly comes to mind? Do you imagine a delicious Big Mac and an order of fries or do you imagine unhealthy fast food? It affects what you choose to purchase. When you think of Federal Express do you think of on-time delivery, or an affordable price, or do you think of something else?

Perception Not Reality

In life, our perception isn't always reality. In branding, it's another story.

When it comes to developing a brand, perception is reality, even when that perception is based on misinformation. What matters is what we believe about a product or a company, despite the facts. Perception is powerful; it affixes a feeling or an experience to a product or company, and that feeling and experience determines all of our actions and reactions to that company now and into the future.

Branding Yourself

While it's important to invest energy in developing your company's brand, it's equally important to develop your personal brand. After all, no matter what your company makes or provides, you're always selling yourself.

The Way You Act is Your Brand

When creating your personal brand, it is important to consider your personality and how it projects the image your customers and prospective customers see.

What we do matters. How we interact with others and the world says a lot about who we are. And in developing a strong personal brand, it's important that your behavior matches the image you want to project.

This doesn't mean you should create a "business you" that looks and sounds like you but acts like someone else. It's always important to be yourself and to stay true to who you are. But if the image you want to create and the person you are do not match, you might want to reconsider your approach. Customers won't want to do business with you if they do not like or trust you. If you aren't true to yourself, your customers will know it. And they'll avoid you at all costs.

The Way You Speak is Your Brand

When developing your personal brand, what you say is just as important as what you do.

The way you act and speak must align with one another. Together, your words and actions form a clear picture in your customers' mind of the kind of person you are. This image is the association that they use to determine if they trust you and if they intend to do business with you.

Don't gossip. Don't badmouth other companies behind their backs. Always try to speak of competitors and clients in a positive light. Make sure the things you say speak positively about you and match the image you're trying to develop.

If your words and actions agree with one another, your customers will think, "Yes, I will do business with them," or "Yes, I will associate myself with this person." If the way you act does not align with the way you speak, those customers will find someone else, because they will not trust you.

The Way You Dress is Your Brand

When developing your personal brand, don't underestimate the power of how you look.

How you dress creates an immediate association in your customer's mind. People are incredibly visual, and we make snap judgments based on how things look. Your customers will decide in an instant, based on how you dress, if you're someone who is a credible projection of your personal brand.

Think about what clothes you choose to wear. Think about the way you choose to groom yourself. Think about the accessories and extras you bring with you when meeting and interacting with a client. They all are part of how customers will perceive who you are and whether doing business with you is worth it.

It's also important to be aware of who your customer is and how he or she dresses. You never want to make a potential customer feel uncomfortable around you. Over-dressing and under-dressing have the potential to create negative associations in your customer's mind about you.

Your personal brand is important. The way you speak, the way you talk, and the way you dress create associations in the mind of your customer, and all three things are part of developing your personal brand. Remember, most people make these associations within the first five seconds. And you never get a second chance to make that first impression.

"Details create the big picture."
– Sanford I. Weill

Details matter. They are a sure giveaway to whether or not you're serious about creating a strong personal brand. So consider the details – they are more important than you think.

Shoes are an important detail to consider, especially when selling or doing business with women. (But don't count out the men. Many men also look at your shoes when making first associations.) Are your shoes shiny? Are your shoes in good shape? Are your shoes of good quality? Do your shoes match your outfit? They don't have to be overly expensive, but good quality shoes are an important detail in personal branding. There's nothing more obvious than someone trying to be something he or she is not, wearing a nice suit or dress with a pair of poor quality, well-worn shoes.

> *"Women notice the shoes."*
> – Adon Rigg

The watch is a very important accessory, particularly for well-to-do men. Women are increasingly picking up on this cue, as well. They will also look at and notice a nice watch. A watch does not need to be expensive or extremely extravagant, but it can be an effective extra touch to your professional image. Some larger retailers sell many watches at an excellent price in comparison to some of the more traditional jewelers you might find in your local shopping center.

Having healthy clean white teeth is an important detail when trying to establish a personal brand. Be aware of your teeth and the things that contribute to staining them, such as coffee, tea, wine, and smoking. Consider getting your teeth whitened. Most dentists offer this service for a nominal fee. There is also an extensive selection of teeth whitening products available at your local pharmacy. You may also consider buying some household low percentage peroxide, mixed with a little water to gargle with in the evenings. You will notice a drastic difference in a matter of days.

Grooming, as a habit, has little to do with affordability and more to do with personal pride.

> *"Nothing is neutral."*
> – Brian Tracy

One of my mentors, Brian Tracy, mentions this often in his books and audio programs. I believe this small, simple statement contains much knowledge and truth. "Nothing is neutral" means everything matters. What you do, what you say, and how you dress contribute positively or negatively to your personal brand and to life in general. Everything counts toward your career, either in your favor or not. Never, ever, ever, does it simply just not matter.

> *"Most people can't tell if you have a $1000 suit or a $400 suit, but they can tell you have a 99 cent BIC pen."*
> – Tim Breithaupt

Questions to Ask Yourself

- What do you *want* your customers to say to others about you?
- What *should* they say about you?
- What *do* they say about you?
- At what can you be best?
- What is your brand presently?

Your Personal Marketing Strategy

Market Yourself

There's no way around it: to be a successful sales person, you ultimately have to sell yourself.

Marketing yourself is a crucial part of developing your personal brand. We're not just talking about business cards and a website. We're talking about developing a concentrated focus on positioning yourself to a specific market segment with the intention of getting those customers to choose you over the many other options out there. It is important to market positively: create positive, not negative, associations in the minds of potential clients or customers. The position you hold in your customers' minds determines all their reactions and interactions with you.

Differentiate Yourself

Your best asset in marketing yourself is what makes you different.

What special attributes do you have that will differentiate yourself from your competition? What do you do that no one else presently does? What can you offer that no one else can offer? Those differences will help you stand out in an already crowded marketplace. So let the differences form the foundation of your personal marketing strategy.

Here are ten ways to differentiate yourself in the minds of your customers. I'm sure you can come up with some of your own. Think outside of conventional wisdom. Think "outside of the box." Develop those unique character traits that will position you positively in the minds of your customer.

1. Build a personal website.
2. Create a Facebook or Twitter page.
3. Be visible within the business community regularly.
4. Create a monthly newsletter.
5. Make consistent phone calls or visits at the same time and place each month.
6. Get published in trade magazines.
7. Participate in speaking engagements.
8. Have superior product and industry knowledge.
9. Have a unique, but professional, style of dress.
10. Positively impact their business. Make them look good. Make them money.

Networking

Networking is a great way to get your name and your business reputation out into the market and establish your personal brand in the business community. There are many different networking groups and events to consider, depending on your type of business. Some groups will be more advantageous to you than others, but all networking can provide some very real benefit to you and your personal Networking should not be about getting customers, but about building relationships. The short-term customer interaction won't develop your business over the long-term, but developing strong, lasting business relationships will. The mark of a true professional is someone with a focus on building relationships, not just the next sale, through the opportunities of networking.

Think of networking like this: you're making deposits into people's lives, not taking withdrawals. Use the law of indirect effort, which I learned from Brian Tracy: you get almost everything out of relationships with others by approaching them indirectly rather than directly. If you want somebody to be impressed with you, first be genuinely impressed with them.

Traditional Networking

Traditional networking means in-person, face-to-face meetings usually held once per month at a convenient location. While not the most popular kind of networking today, traditional networking has its advantages.

Attend traditional networking meetings with a clear focus: only promote one business venture in a given event or meeting. It amazes me how many people go to networking events and describe their involvement in two or more completely different, unrelated businesses. This is the quickest way to position yourself as an amateur business person. The true professional is focused on a singular market segment and committed to building credibility in his or her industry. A true professional knows who her customer is and positions herself to service the customer as the best in the industry. Your goal should be to leave an impression in people's minds that you are knowledgeable, professional, and someone they would do business with and recommend to others.

You probably knew within 30 seconds whether you would date your current partner. Your customer knows in 30 seconds if they will do business with you.

Ten Networking Rules

1. Bring enough business cards.
2. Attend events regularly.
3. Volunteer to be on a committee.
4. Be more interested in other people's businesses before you tell them about yours.
5. Have a 30-second elevator speech which describes who you are and what you do succinctly and imaginatively.
6. After you get the chance to give your elevator speech, ask questions about your networking partner.
7. Ask people to describe their ideal customer: age, sex, height, etc.
8. Recommend either a customer or prospect to them as quickly as possible.
9. Have one unique attribute to differentiate you, e.g., unique tie, shirt, saying.
10. Within 48 hours, contact the other person with a brief "It was a pleasure to meet you," email.

The following are some networking events or ideas to consider.

1. Toastmasters International
2. Trade-related organizations
3. SME I (Sales and Marketing Executives International)
4. Continuing education classes
5. Local industry-related seminars and workshops.

Social Networking

Marketing through Social Media

If someone told you a few years ago that you could reach one billion people from your office, would you have believed him?

Social media has provided us that opportunity to reach many people across the globe with just a click of the computer mouse. To date, Facebook has over 600 million users, Twitter has 175 million users, and LinkedIn is speeding past 100 million users. If you include YouTube with hundreds of millions of users every day, you have at least 1 billion potential customers waiting just beyond your computer screen.

Here's the good news. It's here and it's free.

> *"Social media is the new cold call"*
> – Jeffrey Gitomer

Using Social Media to Position Yourself

The traditional "cold call" was designed to obtain information and make an introduction to a potential customer. It was a simple, cost-effective way of prospecting for new business.

Times were simpler, though, in the age of the cold call. Today, it takes more than just a cold call to connect to the potential customer inundated with information from a variety of media sources. Social media allows you to prospect and build relationships in this new media-rich culture, and it comes at little to no cost from the comfort of your own office.

The one rule of social media marketing: Don't sell; engage.

Let's define social media marketing as a method consisting of either direct or indirect contact, marketing and promotional actions that create awareness and ultimately a purchase of your product or service. This marketing happens by utilizing the Internet and the tools that make the Internet interactive: blogs, vlogs, Twitter, Facebook, LinkedIn, YouTube, and many others.

Social media marketing is about engaging people – your potential customers – by providing excellent, thought-provoking content. The challenge is to create content that will not only excite your followers, but also inspire them to forward your content to their followers, who will hopefully be intrigued to check out your website and eventually become purchasing clients. This platform provides the greatest opportunity for small, medium, and large corporations to build their organizations and create brand awareness.

> *"It's about getting more eyeballs on your brand."*
> – Adon Rigg

Social media marketing is completely different from traditional marketing, so the old rules no longer apply. Traditional marketing was a one-way street, interrupting the consumer's attention to sell a product or service. Social media marketing is a different beast. It doesn't interrupt the consumer; instead, it engages the consumer.

Social media marketing is about people connecting with people, not with a business. People want to engage and build relationships with an intelligent, insightful, thought-provoking individual. They can't really form connections with a product or company. So your social networking strategy begins with your personal brand and the content you create to support your brand. Unique, thought-provoking content on all your social media platforms that support your personal brand will impress potential customers and clients. If they're impressed, they'll forward your material to their friends and colleagues, creating a larger audience of potential connections. More connections mean more opportunities to grow your sales.

Social media marketing provides a great opportunity to stand out from the crowd, but if you're not willing to invest the time and energy to create unique content and consistently engage with others, it might not be a wise investment of your marketing time. Social networking is hard work – you're working to stand out in a crowd of one billion people while driving their behavior through the content you create. But the rewards can be incredible.

Inspire people and engage them with your authenticity. Make the most of the opportunities social media offers.

The Five Ds of Social Media Marketing

Social media is only in its infancy, but we know in just a few short years it has changed the world. The best way to learn the world of social media is to simply dive in – learn what works for you and discover what doesn't. Once you find your place in the world of social media, you'll begin to stand out.

Before you begin your social media campaign, here are five strategic building blocks you should consider.

1) Decide to be relevant.

Staying relevant is important in the world of social media. The best way to be relevant and current is to continue learning what's new in your field of expertise. The world of social media provides a great way to do this. Reading other people's content, books, blogs, and videos will give you an edge on what's new in your industry. A great place to start is Google. It has fantastic tools to assist you in staying informed. Google Reader will import all the blogs you choose, allowing you to gather all your information in one central location. Google alerts will search the Internet for all current web material attached to specific keywords. There are other tools available outside the purpose of this book; you can find more information on them in a suggested reading list at the end of this book.

2) Develop content.

Quality content matters in a good social media marketing campaign. The better your content, the more value you provide to the people who consume that content. Be an active participant in online conversations. Create conversations that center on your business, and the brand you wish to portray. Be consistent in your message and contribute daily or at least weekly. Remember, social media marketing is people-to-people, not business-to-business. You need to ensure that your language is both personable and professional while being honest. Make your social media content an authentic portrayal of whom you really are.

3) Distribute content.

A great way to improve your social media marketing position is to actively distribute the content you create, as well as the content that you read, watch and find of value. Your objective should be to get as many people as possible to view your material. The more people who see you as someone who is connected and a reliable resource, the quicker your database will grow. The simplest way to get your content out in front of the masses is to develop an extensive email database. Your email connections can forward your content by posting a link to your blog via Twitter, LinkedIn, and Facebook. Others will see it, and maybe send it to their friends and colleagues.

4) Discuss the content.

When you discover great content, be sure to comment on the material. This can be as simple as a re-tweet of a link on Twitter or a comment on someone's YouTube video. Engagement is the goal of effective social media marketing, and your ability to create dialogue or a conversation provides you an opportunity to attract advocates to your brand. The more advocates you have, the greater the chance they'll promote and market you to their followers. This kind of engagement will grow your potential audience. An excellent and effective method to discuss content is to participate in group discussions on LinkedIn, which we'll discuss.

5) Duplicate.

The process of good social media marketing is ongoing. Continue to generate great content on a regular basis. Engage in discussions. Connect with your readers and followers. The important thing is to contribute often and have fun.

Again, social media marketing is about engagement with other people. It levels the playing field for all businesses, entrepreneurs, and salespeople and it gives them the ability to build their brand through the content they create. Provided you have the infrastructure to deliver on your promise, you will build and grow brand awareness.

Prospect For New Business

Engaging others will assist you in developing and promoting brand awareness while positioning you as someone who can provide value to prospective customers. The social media platform provides you the opportunity to build trust with those who can purchase your product or service. Trust is developed through the content you provide and through your ability to engage with other like-minded individuals.

Target Market

Social media provides you the ability to "study" target customers and their industry, while learning about prospects, companies, and the competition from the comfort of your own office. There has never been this much opportunity for you to build your brand. But there also have never been so many alternatives for consumers. Look at social media as a way to attract prospects, not as a way to sell something. Building relationships with people who can potentially purchase from you is the primary tool this platform provides. There are almost one billion people online at any given moment; your ability to find those prospects and engage with them provides you an astounding opportunity, but it does not come easily.

Start today

CHAPTER 3 - *The Study Step (Part 2)*
Planning and Preparation

"The readiness is all."

Nothing will get you closer to your goal of a successful sales career more than preparation. In order to connect to potential clients and prove your worth as a professional, preparation matters. The good news is that it's now easier than ever, thanks to the Internet and Web 2.0

Blue Fish Concept

Do you waste your time and resources on accounts that you stand little chance of getting? Are you a "quote and hope" sales person?

Many salespeople were taught to chase any potential lead because sales is a numbers game. The more calls you make the more successful you'll be. Well, sales is no longer a numbers game – that game is over. The cost of doing business is simply too high to pursue any and every opportunity, but the majority of sales people are still being led by those advocating old school cold call and closing techniques.

Activity-based selling no longer produces results. Hardworking salespeople are being forced to sell based on price, because buyers can't differentiate between vendor, product, and services. It therefore places them into commoditization categories, and we all know that price drives commodities.

The high margins that companies experienced in the past are being compressed by the global market and the ability of buyers to find many different alternatives. Sales success now comes from market segmentation and from developing programs, procedures, and products to assist your target market in meeting their goals.

Your Blue Fish or Target Market

What is your blue fish? Your blue fish is the fish (or market) that stands out from all the other goldfish (or industries) in the bowl. When you concentrate on the blue fish, you eliminate all the other accounts that don't have a high need for your product or service.

Your blue fish is the account that complements your organizational strengths and whose needs synchronize with your company's infrastructure. When you focus on the blue fish, you gain an intimate understanding of the challenges they experience. When one has a challenge or unrecognized need for your product or service, the likelihood is that all other blue fish out there have similar challenges.

The S.A.L.E.S. Formula™ will naturally guide you along the process to effectively and efficiently create value for your blue fish and reduce the amount of time required to move them from prospect to customer and, ultimately, to a lifelong client.

Creating long-term clients is the objective of most companies; this can only be achieved by creating value and impacting their profit and loss statement. When you bring this type of value to your clients, you no longer have to rely on heavy discounting to keep their business because you understand your client's industry and the challenges they face.

Blue fish are the only accounts you should spend your time and energy on; your value proposition should be built around their internal and external drivers. This will differentiate you from the competition.

This concept will allow you to experience greater success at a faster rate than you could imagine.

When you identify your blue fish, you are able to develop effective questions that will guide you. Your questions should be centered on their key business drivers that study and research say will impact their business. When you understand your prospect's industry, you can speak their language, and that motivates and creates the desired change.

The blue fish concept allows you to expedite the sales process, sell at higher margins, accomplish more with fewer resources, and provide value to your customers by impacting their bottom line. The remainder of this book is about learning the S.A.L.E.S Formula™, which is to study and become an expert in your customer's industry, ask the questions that identify the pressures that impact your prospect's profitability, and present your solutions in a way that clearly demonstrates the value of doing business with you.

Selling has changed. It's no longer what you sell. It's how you sell.

Become an Industry Expert

To become an expert in your industry, start by determining which industry markets you'd like to focus on. I recommend choosing only one or two industries at first and creating a list of all the companies located in your geographical region. Separate the list into two different categories – one for privately held companies, the other for publicly traded companies. My experience has shown that the culture within publicly traded companies are more open to change and decision makers aren't as determined to protect the incumbent company as in privately held companies.

Prepare your list

To begin, prepare a list of all the companies in the industry of your target market. Complete this list with columns for sales volume, number of employees, number of locations, phone number, address, as well as an area for notes. It might look something like this:

Public	Pvt.	Name	Sales ($)	# of employees	Phone #	Contact	Address	Notes
x		ABC	1,000,000	25	555-5555	Mike W	456 Circle PL	Back November 15th
	x	MNO	2,000,000	43	555-1234	Stephanie K	234 Square St	Call her Tuesday

Before you complete compiling your list, you might want to consider purchasing a Canadian or US business directory. At a cost of a few hundred dollars, these directories provide you with hundreds of thousands of businesses, complete with all the basic information required, such as contact names, phone numbers, email addresses, and much more that will be useful.

What if you do not have the country business directory? A simple yellowpages or Google search will help you identify the names of the companies in your target market area. Once you have developed a list of names, obtain all the information you can about each individual location. The best way to obtain this information is to visit their website and input the information onto your target market list. Studying the industry and target companies will give you a good indication of the potential of the market and whether the investment of your time is worth the potential return.

Where to Find the Information

Now that you have prepared your list of target companies and have determined that this industry will provide you with a positive return on time, you are ready to obtain the information necessary to position and differentiate yourself within this industry as an executive with insight and one who can make a positive impact on your prospect's business.

Industry Blog

A great way to obtain information on a specific industry is to search for blogs from industry experts and set them up on an RSS feed, like Google reader. This allows future blogs to come to you instead of you having to go to them. If you're lucky, you may find a blogger who has been blogging for some time; this could provide you with some valuable information and insight on a particular industry without investing a lot of time searching. A good resource for finding a list of the top blogs in various sectors and industries is www.blogsites.com. It is important to review more than one blog site – you will want to gather many different perspectives and viewpoints on the industry of your choice.

Company Newsletter

Many companies provide newsletters to their customers and investors. Newsletters are a great resource that provides valuable insight into the current status of a company and its industry. Remember we're not only looking for insight, but we're also seeking current events, problems, challenges, and goals the industry or company is experiencing. If one company is having a challenge, the odds are pretty good that many of their competitors are also experiencing the same challenge. Your job is to determine how your product or service can improve their operations or assist them in meeting their goals and objectives.

Company Website

This is obvious, but it needs to be mentioned. A visit to each company's website is imperative. Not only will you learn general information about their company, but you can also gather information about their accomplishments, problems and objectives.

Industry Reports

For a few hundred dollars, you may want to investigate purchasing industry reports by third-party firms. These reports are an excellent information resource which lists all of the players in the industry. It also includes sales figures, industry challenges, and the future outlook for the industry over the next three to five years. A simple Google search or advanced search can increase your odds of finding this information. And www.marketresearch.com is another good resource.

Practice on Smaller Accounts

A great resource for information on the bigger companies can be found in smaller companies within the industry. You can get excellent field practice calling on smaller accounts that won't negatively impact your business if you do not secure them. Small accounts experience the same challenges as large accounts, but a lesser financial penalty is associated with them. If the smaller accounts are having a challenge finding good employees, then the odds are good that the industry in general is also experiencing this challenge. Regardless of the information you're looking for, performing market research on the smaller accounts is a great way to cultivate knowledge to assist you in understanding the market and the standard operating procedures within that sector. Once you have met with three or four of these smaller accounts, trends will begin to appear. This understanding will pave the way to position and differentiate yourself within that industry.

Competition

Know thy enemy, know thyself.

Know your target accounts and gather some first-hand knowledge on what the target industry does. How do they generally operate? What are some challenges they face? Have a game plan to position yourself and your company as one that can make a positive impact on their business. It is important to understand your competitors in as much detail as possible. Knowing what you're up against gives you some critical information that will improve your business prospects.

SWOT Analysis

A SWOT (Strengths, Weaknesses, Opportunities, Threats) analysis is a tool used by many executives to gain a more detailed understanding of the competition. It will show how they measure up to your own company. It is important to not rely on your opinion only, as this may be a little biased. Your objective is to obtain reliable and valuable information as you do not want any surprises once you launch your campaign.

A SWOT analysis consists of the strengths, weaknesses, opportunities, threats. Here's a visual representation to assist you:

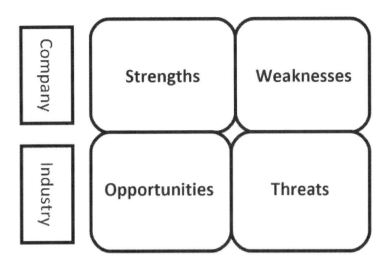

The following comes from Wikipedia which gives you a detailed explanation of what a SWOT analysis is all about:

SWOT analysis is a strategic planning method used to evaluate the Strengths, Weaknesses, Opportunities, and Threats involved in a project or in a business venture. It involves specifying the objective of the business venture or project and identifying the internal and external factors that are favourable and unfavourable to achieve that objective. The technique is credited to Albert Humphrey, who led a convention at Stanford University in the 1960s and 1970s using data from Fortune 500 companies.

A SWOT analysis must first start with defining a desired end state or objective. A SWOT analysis may be incorporated into the strategic planning model. Strategic Planning, including SWOT and SCAN analysis, has been the subject of much research.

- Strengths: internal attributes of the person or company that are helpful to achieving the objective(s).

- Weaknesses: internal attributes of the person or company that are harmful to achieving the objective(s).

- Opportunities: external conditions that are helpful to achieving the objective(s).

- Threats: external conditions which could do damage to the objective(s).

Identification of SWOTs is essential because subsequent steps in the process of planning for achievement of the selected objective may be derived from the SWOTs.

First, the decision makers have to determine whether the objective is attainable, given the SWOTs. If the objective is NOT attainable a different objective must be selected and the process repeated. The SWOT analysis is often used in academia to highlight and identify strengths, weaknesses, opportunities, and threats. It is particularly helpful in identifying areas for development.

Marketing Using SWOT

In many competitor analyses, marketers build detailed profiles of each competitor in the market, focusing especially on their relative competitive strengths and weaknesses using SWOT analysis. Marketing managers will examine each competitor's cost structure, sources of profits, resources and competencies, competitive positioning and product differentiation, degree of vertical integration, historical responses to industry developments, and other factors.

Marketing management often finds it necessary to invest in research to collect the data required to perform accurate marketing analysis. Accordingly, management often conducts market research (alternately marketing research) to obtain this information. Marketers employ a variety of techniques to conduct market research, but some of the more common include:

- Qualitative marketing research, such as focus groups
- Quantitative marketing research, such as statistical surveys
- Experimental techniques, such as test markets
- Observational techniques, such as ethnographic (on-site) observation
- Marketing managers may also design and oversee various environmental scanning and competitive intelligence processes to help identify trends and inform the company's marketing analysis.

Below is an example using SWOT to analyze the market position of a small management consultancy with specialism in HRM.

Strengths	Weaknesses	Opportunities	Threats
Reputation in marketplace	Shortage of consultants at operating level rather than partner level	Well established position with a well defined market niche	Large consultancies operating at a minor level
Expertise at partner level in HRM consultancy	Unable to deal with multidisciplinary assignments because of size or lack of ability	Identified market for consultancy in areas other than HRM	Other small consultancies looking to invade the marketplace

Once you have completed a SWOT analysis of the competition, you're ready for the last piece of the planning puzzle.

The Competition's Account Manager

It is important to obtain as much information as possible on the account manager (or whatever equitable role performs those basic functions). I want to be extremely clear: we are searching for information on the professional skills of the competitor's sales force. We are not interested – nor should we EVER be – in their personal lives. Understanding the competitive sales professional helps you know when and where to pick your battles.

If the account you want to call on is privately held, the competition very strong, or the account manager has been around for many years, it may be a challenge. Obtaining that account may require much more strategic planning than if your competitor were weaker than your company or has a brand-new rep in the territory. If your target account is publicly traded or facing some financial pressure with a brand new contact person, there might be a completely different scenario. Your return on effort and return on time are important factors to consider here, and understanding your competitors will aid this. Knowing how to balance this is the mark of a true professional executive.

Some of the resources you may want to use to gather competitive information on the account manager are:

Existing prospects – Accounts you are calling on who purchase from your competitors are a great resource to obtain useful information. Simply asking your contact about the competition will paint a clear picture of the sales rep, because the rep in many circumstances is the face of the company. First-hand comments will tell you a great deal about how the competition is positioned with that company.

Industry contacts – People have opinions, and they usually will share them when asked. Therefore ask customers, colleagues, and even your boss. This does not need to be complicated. Nothing more than, "I have heard great things about (whomever) from our competition. Do you know him?"

CHAPTER 4 - *The Study Step (PART 3)*
Prospecting

Push /Pull Strategy

In a business context Push-Pull describes the movement of a product or information between two subjects. In the marketplace the consumers usually "pull" the goods or information they need, while suppliers "push" them toward the consumers. In supply chains the stages are operating normally both in a "push" and "pull" manner. Push production is based on forecast demand and pull production is based on actual or consumed demand. The interface between these stages is called the push-pull boundary, or decoupling point.

In today's new internet and social media based economy, the lines between marketing and sales are becoming more entwined and the importance of generating a pull versus push strategy becomes that much more important to building a sustainable customer base.

The Study portion of the S.A.L.E.S Formula is designed around positioning, planning, and prospecting to assist you in creating and developing your own personal brand. Over time the need to push your product or service onto the consumer will diminish as you should be building your brand and creating a pull strategy. The "push/pull" concept is central to marketing. Pull marketing is when customers are waiting to purchase what you're selling with little or no effort on the company's part. Think of the Apple iPhone. When it was first released, people were lined up outside of Apple stores waiting to be one of a hundred people who would be the first to have it. Push marketing is when the product is pushed through distribution to the consumer. In this concept, distribution needs to train their sales force, print a bunch of brochures and pound the pavement looking for customers to push the product to.

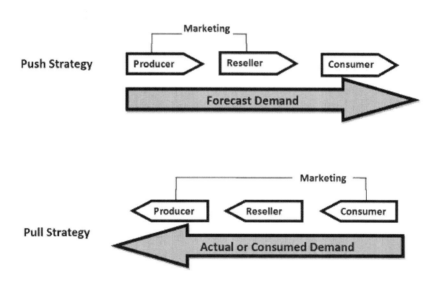

Marketing

Push Strategy

Another meaning of the push strategy in marketing can be found in the communication between seller and buyer. In dependence of the used medium, the communication can be either interactive or non-interactive. For example, if the seller makes his promotion by television or radio, it's not possible for the buyer to interact with. On the other hand, if the communication is made by phone or internet, the buyer has possibilities to interact with the seller. In the first case information is just "pushed" toward the buyer, while in the second case it is possible for the buyer to demand the needed information according to his requirements.

- Applied to that portion of the supply chain where demand uncertainty is relatively small
- Production & distribution decisions are based on long term forecasts
- Based on past orders received from retailer's warehouse (may lead to Bullwhip effect)
- Inability to meet changing demand patterns
- Large and variable production batches
- Unacceptable service levels
- Excessive inventories due to the need for large safety stocks
- Less expenditure on advertising than pull strategy

Pull Strategy

In a marketing "pull" system the consumer requests the product and "pulls" it through the delivery channel. An example of this is the car manufacturing company Ford Australia. Ford Australia only produces cars when they have been ordered by the customers.

- Applied to that portion of the supply chain where demand uncertainty is high
- Production and distribution are demand driven
- No inventory, response to specific orders

- Point of sale (POS) data comes in handy when shared with supply chain partners
- Decrease in lead time
- Difficult to implement

Supply chains

With a push-based supply chain, products are pushed through the channel, from the production side up to the retailer. The manufacturer sets production at a level in accord with historical ordering patterns from retailers. It takes longer for a push-based supply chain to respond to changes in demand, which can result in overstocking or bottlenecks and delays (the bullwhip effect), unacceptable service levels and product obsolescence.

In a pull-based supply chain, procurement, production and distribution are demand-driven rather than to forecast. However, a pull strategy does not always require make-to-order production. Toyota Motors Manufacturing is frequently used as an example of pull production; yet do not typically produce to order. They follow the "supermarket model" where limited inventory is kept on hand and is replenished as it is consumed. In Toyota's case, Kanban cards are used to signal the need to replenish inventory.

A supply chain is almost always a combination of both push and pull, where the interface between the push-based stages and the pull-based stages is sometimes known as the push–pull boundary.[5] However, because of the subtle difference between pull production and make-to-order production a more accurate name for this may be the decoupling point. An example of this would be Dell's build to order supply chain. Inventory levels of individual components are determined by forecasting general demand, but final assembly is in response to a specific customer request. The decoupling point would then be at the beginning of the assembly line.

Death of the Cold Call

Cold calling is dead. It's an old-school concept, and today it's considered the mark of an amateur. Professional executives do not need the cold call in a world of other, more sophisticated options.

For clarification, cold calling is defined as: walking into someone's place of business without an appointment and expecting to meet them and sell them something right then and there. It doesn't work anymore. Leave it behind.

Prospecting in the 21ˢᵗ Century: Five Steps to Prospecting with Social Media

> "Social media is the new cold call."
> – Jeffery Gitomer

Connecting with buyers is challenging. The average businessperson receives more than 50 emails per day, and buyers are simply too busy to respond to someone they don't know trying to sell them something they perceive they don't need.

Ask yourself: do you respond or even read emails from someone you don't know? Let's be honest – we all press the delete button.

I strongly suggest purchasing one of the many great books available on social media and gain a more thorough understanding of its power. Until then, here are five steps to effective prospecting using social media.

1) Identify your blue fish.

Using the various social media networks, find which of your target prospects (blue fish) is participating in social media. What groups does she belong to? How many connections away are you from her on LinkedIn? Do you have a mutual connection who can introduce you?

2) Follow.

Once you've found her, you need to follow her. Does she blog? What books does she recommend? What hobbies does she participate in? What character traits does she seem to possess? Is she a relater, driver, analyzer, expresser? (We will discuss personality types in further chapters.)

3) Study them.

Follow your prospect for a minimum of two weeks, reading all her blogs, tweets, posts, videos, and any recent books she has suggested

before you proceed to step four. Should you determine her to be a relater or expresser personality, consider learning about her hobbies. If she is an avid golfer, gain an understanding of the game and learn who the top players in the game of golf are. Who won the Masters Tournament? This all takes time, but it's free and will increase your likelihood of success.

4) Connect with them.

Social media has made prospecting to buyers easier than ever before. Social media forces people to respond, because the communication is out in the open for all other networkers to see. This platform promotes professional behavior, and people notice if you have not responded to someone's comments. Remember, everyone is a brand, and no one can afford to have his or her brand tarnished. Responding is good social media etiquette.

Connecting with someone is a simple process, and can be as easy as "liking" someone's Facebook page or commenting on her wall. It can also be as simple as re-tweeting a link or providing a provoking thought or opinion on Twitter. If she asks a question in a social media group, provide an answer. People notice when you respond to their questions. Everyone appreciates the attention and recognition -- it makes us feel good and we all like to have our egos stroked.

Respond to people's questions through LinkedIn or join groups that your prospect participates in. Comment on questions that members in the group are asking. The more you participate and provide insightful opinions, thoughts, or perspectives, the more value you provide and the more you will be recognized.

Prospecting through social media is a much simpler process than traditional cold calling, and the success rate is much higher. In fact as a LinkedIn paid monthly member, through your Inmail, you can connect with any potential buyer, and if someone does not respond to your request for a meeting, you are not charged for that request in your monthly Inmail allowance.

5) Make contact.

Depending on the social media platform you're working with, connecting with prospects is accomplished in different ways. Each one has a different protocol for making contact with other members. You can direct message someone who's following you on Twitter, and with Facebook you can like someone's business page. On LinkedIn, you can ask someone you know to introduce you to the prospective buyer. Regardless of the format you use, reach out to the individual and make the connection real. Always respect social media etiquette, and the rules that each platform has in place.

The Importance of Your Website

Anyone who may be interested in doing business with you and your company is eventually going to visit your website. Everything you do in social media marketing to create and build your brand links back to your content; the majority of your content will be located at your website. Your website is a window into what your company is like from the buyer's perspective; therefore, it is important that you have an excellent website. People judge other people based on their websites just as they judge your appearance in person-to-person contact.

When having your website developed, ask yourself the crucial question: what is my brand? You should be able to answer this question in one word. Don't make the mistake many people do in trying to be everything. What one word do you want people to use when they describe your brand or business? What do you want people to think of when they do business with you? When they visit your website, what words do you want them to think about? Are you in the business of social media, law firm, sales and marketing, leadership, interior design, accounting, cleaning? If you are a law firm, what kind of law do you specialize in? Is it child custody, divorce, impaired driving, trademarks and licensing? If it's a cleaning company, what kind of cleaning company are you? Are you commercial, residential, retail, industrial, green?

What do you help other people achieve? There should be only one thing in which you specialize. That will differentiate and position you as an expert in the mind of the buyer. These are the things that create a brand, and that's what your website should express when potential buyers visit.

The Five Musts of an Effective Website

Appearance – Your website is a window into your company; the design of the site must align with the image you want to portray. Does your website complement your business? Do they look alike? Are they the same colors? Does the logo match? Your website needs to have features such as a link to your Twitter, Facebook, and LinkedIn pages. Your blog should be visible and easy for all to view. Look at your competitor's website, and see what you like and what you don't. Add those features you like and incorporate them into your site. A strong, clear visual aesthetic is an essential component in developing a good website that invites people to stay beyond the first click.

Layout – A confused mind will always say, "No." The layout and design of your website must be pleasing to the eye and easy to navigate. Finding information that the visitor requires should be an easy and intuitive process. Remember that less is more when developing a website. What feeling do you want to convey to the visitor? Does your website evoke this feeling?

Information – Your website must provide excellent content and information. Your objective is to educate the viewer and position you as an expert. It's one thing to have excellent content, and another to have viewers view that content. You should consider the different ways people receive information: through sight, sound, feeling, smell, and taste.

Whenever possible, implement these different senses into your website or any other time you are providing information and trying to influence behavior. Consider using both text and video. Many people watch the video and print the text to review at a later time as a resource.

Don't let the idea of video intimidate you. Creating video has never been easier and can be done very effectively from your own smartphone. If you still feel uncertain about creating video, you can always hire someone to assist you at very competitive rates through websites such as elance.com. You should be aware of the potential drawback to video: the longer your video, the lower the viewership. Over 75% of viewers are no longer watching your video after two minutes, and 50% have dropped off after one minute of viewing.

Blogs are a great method of providing excellent content. Search engines like Google look for that content in ranking your site, therefore the more content you provide, the more information the search engines have to draw from. This improves your ranking and they'll consider your site more relevant to the searcher's request.

Collect data – "What gets measured gets done," is a famous managerial phrase. Your website should be no different. The collection of email addresses is a great way to start. The more addresses you have, the greater the potential audience you'll have to market your goods and services. Create a newsletter program that allows you to measure the numbers of people who opt out and of people who open your email. This is a great way to determine whether or not people are viewing your content. Programs like Google Analytics provide you with the data necessary to determine which keywords are being used to find your website.

The collection of data is an important resource in determining your return on effort and the return on your investment and time. Any good web designer will have an in-depth knowledge of the tools available to grow your database and maximize your conversion rate. An effective website must entice people to navigate around your site. The information or content motivates them to return again and again. The collection of data allows you to measure the behavior of these visitors and whether they are being converted into customers.

Update – The final step is transforming your customers into clients by continually updating your website with new information. Regularly update your website with excellent content in the form of new blogs, video and anything relevant to your business. Incorporate features like newsletters, polls, and surveys without compromising your brand.

Remember: What is it that you want people to think when they visit your website? Are you accomplishing this goal?

Five Social Media Sites You Need to Know

YouTube: Your Own Television Channel for Free

Participating in social media allows you to prospect, position, market, and sell your product or service to over one billion people. It was challenging to determine whether this section should be placed under positioning, planning, or prospecting, because each of these five social media platforms assist you in all three categories. Social media allows you to achieve all three effectively, efficiently, and (aside from the time you invest in it) freely 24 hours a day, seven days per week.

The Golden Rule to social media for business: content is king. Your primary objective is to educate and engage those who interact with you. There is no shortage of outlets where people can obtain information, but most people don't know where to start finding that information. When they develop a relationship with you, trust is established. You are then positioned in the mind of the prospect as a reliable resource for quality content and information.

YouTube allows you to have your own television channel for free while marketing that channel to one billion people. If It weren't real, it would sound too good to be true. YouTube is a place for people to get information; in fact, it is a place for people to watch information. YouTube is the second largest search engine behind Google and has thousands of new videos added every day. From a marketing and positioning standpoint, you should make YouTube a part of your strategy.

Once you upload content to your channel, it's easy to post links of your material via Facebook, LinkedIn, and Twitter. Studies show that people retain 10% of the information they read, but more than 50% of what they watch. People retain information better through visual means, so video can connect to new customers or clients in amazing ways.

When producing a video, remember that the attention span of people these days is extremely short. Research suggests that within:

10 seconds you lose 10% of your audience
30 seconds you lose 30% of your audience
1 minute and you lose 50% of your audience
2 minutes you lose over 75% of your audience

The following are five YouTube musts to creating loyal viewership:

Differentiate – If you don't differentiate in business, you are just a commodity. So you need to stand out from the crowd. The way to do this is to provide more value to your viewers than the competition provides. This can be done in the way of content, insight, humor, likability – you're only limited by your own imagination. The bottom line is: In business, if you don't differentiate, you die.

Specialization – What do you do best? You can be a jack of all trades but you'll be a master of none. What do you want to be known for? Is it sales, marketing, HR, art, mechanics? Whatever your passionate is about, and what you want to be known for, is the brand you should be creating.

Segmentation – Who is your target market? Who is your most likely customer? What are the characteristics of the potential viewers you want to reach? Who do you feel qualified to teach? What age are they? What sex are they? What income bracket? Once you have answered these questions clearly, it should be your primary aim to please the viewer better than any of your competitors.

Focus – Once you've identified your target market, do everything in your power to serve and provide value to that market segment. Remember: avoid the status quo. Do not become complacent, because people's tastes change over time. It is important to stay connected to their changing needs, wants, and desires. Keep them engaged and turn them into promoters of your brand.

Schedule – Part of developing a successful brand is being consistent. If you create content on a weekly basis, be sure to have new content uploaded the same time and day every week. If it's daily, be sure to provide new content every day. Failure to be consistent with your programming will prevent you from creating the loyalty that you're working so hard to build.

As the younger generation matures, video will become more mainstream and an integral part of marketing and communicating. The younger generation reads less and certainly not to the degree of other generations. The majority of the world's population is presently under the age of 25. They use social media on a daily basis. In fact, they do not know a world without the computer.

If you have not embraced video as part of your marketing, you're missing out on a key tool of the sales professional of the future.

Facebook for Business

Facebook is an excellent resource for business-to-consumer (or B2C) engagement. With 600 million members, half of which log in each day, you cannot ignore the power and influence of Facebook. There are three different pages that can be created on Facebook: a profile page, a fan page, and the group page.

We will look at each of these individually.

Profile Page

The profile page is an individual page on Facebook. This is the page that people use to share their personal lives, and it's a place where friends and families connect, and share pictures and memories. A person you have confirmed as a friend can comment on your wall, and you can upload video, join groups, and play games. Your connections can view your page at his leisure. You have the ability to make your page public for all to see, semi-private (where only certain segments of your page can be viewed), or completely private (where no one can view anything unless he or she is a friend and you have given permission to connect).

Group page

The Facebook group page can be created by any member and can either be inclusive (open to the public) or exclusive (by invitation and permission only). Group owners can send up to 500 e-mails at one time, and members can respond to messages sent by the group administrator. Members can participate in conversations, exchange content – much like any person-to-person networking group.

Business page

The business page was designed for businesses to have space to build their brand presence. Your Facebook business page can have an unlimited number of fans and is indexed by search engines, which allows for high ranking and optimization through Google, Yahoo, and other search engines. You can update your status from this page, as well as provide information about your company in the information section or you can utilize many other communication tools that are available. From your Facebook page you can share a link allowing others to easily view your information. You can also invite others to become fans, which is a great way to market yourself and build your fan base.

Once you hit 25 fans, or "LIKES", you can obtain a username for your page, which provides you with a more complete, branded look. You have the ability to create an event and promote that event with a Facebook event page. You can invite friends, family, and prospects who can also invite people they know to your event, while collecting and confirming attendance. Facebook indexes your event as well, which means search engines can find it, allowing for higher potential viewership. These events can range from local gatherings, concerts, recitals, book signings, webinars, seminars, workshops, meetings, and new product launches.

Marketing Your Business with Your Facebook Page

Different tools and features are available to assist you in marketing your business. These tools help you promote your page and build relationships with other Facebook users. The tabs that appear on your Facebook page are standard. They allow people to easily navigate around your page and include items such as blog tab, note tab, slide share, and others.

Many third-party participants have developed applications to help you promote your business. These applications provide you an opportunity to engage your community more efficiently. Some of these applications include:

Marketplace: In this application you can buy, sell, and search for whatever you wish.

Eventbrite: this application helps promote events and sell tickets. It also will track responses to invitations.

My LinkedIn: Add this tab to your profile page, which shows your limited profile to others.

E-commerce store: With this application, you can run a store or provide the ability to process payments on your Facebook page.

Sign-up form: With this application you can gather visitor information.

Social tweet: Link Twitter to your Facebook, and Facebook to your Twitter account. When you post on one platform, it is displayed on the other.

These are just a few examples of what you can do to build your business and engage customers in an effort to build your brand. There are 600 million Facebook users; 300 million users (the equivalent to the population of the USA) visit and engage in one form or another every single day. When a member on Facebook chooses to like your page, then your business is visible to their friends. Presently the average user has 114 friends. Therefore with just 100 people liking your business page, you have the potential to interact, engage, attract, and sell to 11,400 new consumers. And it's all in your hands for free.

Twitter for Business

Twitter is easy, fun, and free. It truly is a person-to-person network that allows you to meet, connect, and engage with like-minded individuals. Because you can only tweet 140 characters at a time, the Twitter platform is often referred to as "micro-blogging," and it provides you with the opportunity to build your brand one tweet at a time.

Once you sign up and obtain a user name, you can begin to connect with others immediately. It is important to remember that you are building a brand which may be either personal or business, so carefully consider everything you tweet. Your messages will either position you in the light you intend or they won't. The good news is that you're only limited by your own imagination.

Once you begin to follow someone on Twitter, his or her tweets appear in your home screen updates. When someone follows you, all your thoughts and tweets appear on his or her homepage. Many people download a Twitter application for their smartphones for more mobile access to Twitter, and many phones come with the application already loaded for you, making it convenient and fun.

It takes time to build a Twitter following, so you should consider quality versus quantity of followers. Just because you have 1000 followers doesn't mean that 1000 people are paying attention to your tweets. Follow people you find interesting and who have enjoyable content.

Follow only people whom you can learn from and engage with.
To get started, follow these steps:

1) Sign up: Once you get to the Twitter page, choose the sign-link. Enter the required information and choose your user name carefully. I recommend using your personal name if it is available. You'll want to ensure that your user name aligns and complements the brand you're trying to build. Your user name will be visible to everyone when you post a tweet or when someone retweets your tweets, so don't take this step lightly. Potentially, millions can see your micro-blog.

2) Edit your profile: Upload your image (or your "avatar") into your profile description, explaining your business or value proposition. Customize your Twitter background with your company colors or picture that complements your brand. There are many websites that assist you with this for free or for a nominal fee. It's important to remember that Twitter is really a person-to-person network, and people do not want to connect, engage, and interact with a company or logo. They do want to interact with a down-to-earth, personable, and insightful individual.

3) Start tweeting: Begin posting great thoughts, ideas, insights, opinions, or advice. There is a general consensus that you should follow the 80/20 rule – 80% of your tweets should be content-based, and 20% should be promoting or selling your product or service. Again, nobody is going to want to read or interact if all you're doing is promoting and advertising. But when you post great content, people will notice. So when you tweet about your brand, they will connect your content with your product or service.

4) Follow others: Follow people you find interesting and who you think might be able to provide insight and value to you. It doesn't matter if you know someone or not. You can follow anyone. Just don't expect someone to follow you just because you follow them. Don't worry about quantity of followers. Simply provide great content and follow those who interest you. By providing interesting and informative content, you will build your followers.

5) Don't stop: Tweet every day and tweet often. Twitter is much like a real-life friendship – the more you interact, the more the relationship grows. Consider creating a list of thoughts and insights in a separate notebook, and then from time to time throughout the day, tweet those thoughts regularly and consistently. But always tweet something consistent with the brand you're trying to build.

What to tweet

Twitter is an excellent platform to build awareness of your business and to create a brand. Tweet anything and everything that you want to share, as long as it is consistent with your brand identity. It can become a challenge to post a tweet that has clarity while being limited to just 140 characters, but this is what makes it both challenging and fun.
The list below contains ideas to help you begin tweeting and engaging others while building your brand.

Future plans – What's coming up in your life? Is there an anniversary or birthday? Twitter is a tool for you to build your brand, but it is a person-to-person network first and foremost. People don't want to connect with the product, but they are looking to engage with real and interesting people.

"What are you doing?" – For the record, nobody cares that you are about to brush your teeth. But they might find it interesting that you are at the Super Bowl, or the sold-out concert in town. Let people know when you're doing something exciting, because they will probably be excited for you.

Share – When you find a great article or other kinds of interesting content, share a link to that article, blog, video, or picture. It doesn't always have to be original content. It's okay to share other people's thoughts and content, provided you always give credit where credit is due. When someone tweets something interesting, retweet it to your followers. Both you and the original tweeter will be appreciative.

Ask – If you want to know something, just ask. This is a simple thing to do and some of the responses to your question can be most interesting and insightful.

Tweet when you've completed something – Have you just finished watching a fantastic game? Tweet that. "What a goal!" or "What an exciting game!" can be ways to start a discussion. Remember: engage, share and connect.

Inform – Give advice and insight, or share ideas that can improve your followers' business or simply try to improve someone's life in some way.

Be yourself. Provide excellent content. Engage others. You'll position yourself as someone whom others recognize has something of value to give.

Now start tweeting.

LinkedIn: Business to Business Social Network

With over 90 million users, LinkedIn provides an opportunity that many people simply have yet to discover. This platform is the foundation for business-to-business social media, and for those in the sales profession, this is where the majority of your social media time will be best served.

LinkedIn is an all-business network that allows you to generate leads and differentiate yourself from the crowd, while giving you the ability to position yourself and create awareness of your expertise. LinkedIn is the Rolodex for the 21st Century, providing the opportunity to make lifelong friendships, share ideas, and learn from others in your profession.

Prospecting with LinkedIn

LinkedIn is the simplest process for those in sales providing you the ability to prospect, attract, and connect with buyers at an unprecedented speed. LinkedIn is much more than an online resume, but it will only benefit you if you participate and engage with those in your network. LinkedIn is a prospecting tool that can fill your pipeline quickly while giving you access to buyers, executives, and decision makers within moments. These contacts are even more accessible when you subscribe to LinkedIn's monthly paid subscription, which provides you with Inmail (LinkedIn e-mail) and other ways to engage and connect with prospects who are not currently in your network. By maximizing these features you will grow and expand your Rolodex at a more rapid pace.

LinkedIn really is what you make of it, and your ability to connect with others will be determined by how effectively you give people a reason to connect with you. This is established by understanding and utilizing the segments that will make your LinkedIn experience more valuable.

The segments are:

1) **LinkedIn Profile**

   A.   To participate in LinkedIn, you'll need to set up your profile. If you're using LinkedIn for business, you will need to ensure your profile settings are configured to make you visible to the public. An active profile allows you to leverage the tools and applications to create awareness of yourself and your business. This awareness begins with your profile page. Everyone looks to see the number of connections you have; therefore growing the number of connections you have provides a higher perception of your individual value.

B.   You grow your connection base by being engaged with participants and consciously building your network one connection at a time. When you meet someone in person, ask him to join your network. The great news is that everyone else is looking to build his base and will be more than happy to connect with you to build his own network connection numbers. When seeking a connection, always personalize the message. Refrain from using the standard default message, as this can be seen as insincere and formal. It only takes a moment to add that personal touch.

You will also want to build the number of recommendations you have; however, you want to consider a couple of things before you request a recommendation from those in your network.

- The demographic and psychographic of those reading your recommendations.

- How you want to be positioned and perceived by those who read your recommendations.

The recommendations that provide the greatest value to you are those from people who have had experience working with you. The best way to gather recommendations is to ask those who are in your network to recommend you. There is no need to worry about the wording people use in your recommendation, because LinkedIn allows you to choose whether to display or hide each individual recommendation.

C.   Your summary statement should be well written and explain your experience and what value you've provided to past employers. If you are in sales or are attempting to position yourself as an expert in your field, then make your summary statement about your mission and how those dealing with you will benefit from their interaction with you. Consider the

LinkedIn groups you belong to as this provides insight into your personality and interests. Do they demonstrate professionalism and align with your personal brand?

Finally, connect your LinkedIn account with Twitter. To do this, go to "edit profile" on your LinkedIn home page, and click "add twitter account." Configure your account to integrate with LinkedIn.

2) LinkedIn Answers

This section is where you can position yourself as an expert, differentiate your personal brand, and increase your connections. Answers provide an excellent opportunity to find members who have asked a question related to your industry and the product or service you represent. When you respond to a question someone has asked, this allows you to showcase your business name and create awareness of your brand. When you correspond with another member by responding to answers, be sure to make a connection request to build your network base.

3) LinkedIn Groups

Groups is an excellent way to find other like-minded members with similar interests. Once you find a group that interests you, join that group and participate in the discussion. You may join up to 50 different groups, but I suggest that first you join no more than five groups. This will allow you to participate without getting overwhelmed or lost in the process. When you're a member of a group, you can contact members without needing to upgrade to a paid subscription. When you're considering joining a group, look at the number of members they have. This can be a great prospecting tool for you. But join groups judiciously – you don't want to be labelled as someone who joins groups to spam others. Everything you do is either working positively or negatively to build your brand.

Create your own group

Creating a group is easy to set up, but it takes work and dedication to build that group's membership base. As a group owner, you will be responsible for asking questions and maintaining the flow of the group discussion. There are many benefits to creating a group, and one of them is that you position yourself as a person of influence. This can be amplified by posting great content, sharing links to excellent material, and asking thought-provoking questions. Another benefit to owning a group is that you can communicate directly with all members regardless of whether you have a personal connection with them or not.

4) **LinkedIn Events**

Similar to Facebook events, LinkedIn allows you to create and post upcoming events like conferences, gatherings and open houses. It's a great way to promote your business and build awareness of your brand.

5) **Participation**

LinkedIn, like other social networks, is very user-friendly. It doesn't take long to become comfortable with the network. Don't be intimidated. Begin by setting up a profile and reaching out to people in your immediate circle. There are many great books that can help you become more comfortable with LinkedIn if you feel you need assistance. Establish a schedule to ensure you participate regularly – it doesn't need to be any more than five or ten minutes a day.

Sales 2.0

As discussed at the beginning of this book, Sales 2.0 uses the power of technology to create, develop, and serve the customer. With all the tools available via the Internet, this goal should be easily accomplished. The Internet should be a vital part of your prospecting system because of its ease, simplicity, and affordability.

To review from Chapter 1:

What is Sales 2.0? It is the use of innovative sales practices, focused on creating value for both the buyer and seller and enabled by Web 2.0 and next generation technology. Sales 2.0 practices combining the science of process driven operations with the art of collaborative relationships, using the most profitable and most expedient sales resources required to meet customers' needs. This approach produces superior, predictable, repeatable business results, including increased revenue, decreased costs, and sustained competitive advantage. It is the practice of inter-related interdependent categories: strategy, people, process, and technology.

Strategy - Your most experienced and expensive sales team should be focused on your largest qualified customers or sales opportunities. You can leverage their time and attention with a sales strategy that includes sales resources dedicated to sales opportunities that don't require face-to-face interaction. Sales 2.0 leverages the most expensive sales reps while keeping sales pipeline consistently full, increasing customer acquisition and revenue generation, which keep cost of sales low to deliver maximum value to investors and shareholders.

People: Are focused on building relationships with customers and peers. These open-minded reps use the phone and web extensively in place of on-site visits to contain costs, improve productivity, and provide more immediate service. Team selling goals and individual goals are supported by compensation plans that reward Sales 2.0 behavior.

Process: Sales 2.0 process is designed with customers at the forefront and asks: What are their business initiatives? What action must they take at each step? What do they need from you and by when? Are you easy to do business with? This customer-focused process gives you a framework by which to measure your business metrics and key performance indicators (KPIs) to figure out what's working and what's not. Without it you can't predict business results.

Technology: The predictable, constant improvement in business processes, and strong, engaged online relationships that are the hallmark of sales 2.0 are supported by technology. It may be customer relationship management (CRM), business analytics, e-mail, and web site tracking software, or products that accelerate account research or lead generation that help make sales reps more effective and efficient. Or it may be video e-mail, webinar software, or sales portals that encourage interaction, collaboration, and engagement. Without today's technology enabling detailed sales process measurement and analysis – as well as building meaningful relationships without in-person meetings – Sales 2.0 simply wouldn't be possible.

Contract Out

With the tools available on the Internet, businesses and executives should consider contracting out the telemarketing/telesales department to generate leads. Meanwhile, you can focus your time turning those leads into customers and clients.

Once you have a database of prospects created through networking, the next step is to hire a professional to approach and develop those prospects. This will provide you with a warm call and a booked appointment. There are many companies that specialize in telesales that are highly qualified to generate that appointment. Once you begin networking, you will undoubtedly meet top-quality people in the business of generating appointments. I personally like dealing with small business owners who specialize in this market. In my experience, they are more personal and personable to deal with and are better at becoming an extension of your business. A smart collaboration with a small company will offer your prospects a better glimpse into your company culture. This will save you both time and money.

This is not to say that using a large professional company will not provide the same personal touch. One Google search using the word "telesales" provides over 14,000,000 results. I suspect you might find the right fit with one or more of these companies.

CRM (Customer Relationship Management)

37,900,000.

That's how many customer relationship management (CRM) programs can be found in one Google search.

A CRM program can either be a valuable tool or it can be a "make work" project. I personally use one that helps me build relationships and differentiate myself: Jeffery Gitomer's Ace of Sales program (www.aceofsales.com).

It allows me to send Facebook, Twitter, and LinkedIn updates, send branded emails, thank you or get well cards and ecards, track emails, import contacts, create a strategy file, send e-zines, and much more. Depending on your needs, there are many excellent CRM programs available, all of which provide a dashboard to see the potential projects in the hopper complete with an estimated dollar figure associated with each account. Most programs allow you to run an email marketing campaign from within the system.

Why do I have CRM information in a discussion on prospecting? With the Internet and Web 2.0 tools, the distinction between marketing and sales becomes less clear. Regardless of the program you use, choose one and begin creating and cultivating relationships.

> *"What you lack in marketing must be made up in sales."*
> – Kathy Heasley

Trade Shows

Trade shows are a great way to generate warm leads with interested potential customers. But don't waste the opportunity. Standing in your booth with a look of "Pick me! Pick me!" won't be effective. Think outside the box to draw interest for you and your company.

I know one trade show booth representative who offered popcorn he'd pop on site. Maybe offering ice cream cones or free giveaways could be innovative ways to get people connected to your trade show booth.

Don't be afraid to leave your booth and seek out opportunities. This requires an outgoing personality and a smile, but it works very effectively, especially if you create a reason for people to come back to your booth. Hand out an enticing raffle form that requires them to fill out and drop off at your booth. People are inundated with information at trade shows, and someone is always trying to sell them something. You need to have the attitude of Heather Kardel CEO of Professional Fish Career Profiles: "Dive in and stand out."

The Benefit of Networking and Selling to the C-Suite

"Selling to the C-Suite" is a great book by authors Nicholas A.C. Read and Stephen J. Bistrite. In their book, they examine excellent research performed with C-level executives. What did they discover? The most effective way to gain access to this level executive is from a recommendation by someone else in the executive's company. Their research indicates that 82% of executives said they would usually or always grant a meeting with a sales person who was recommended internally.

	Always	Usually	Occasionally	Never
Recommendations from someone in your company.	16%	68%	16%	0%
Referral from someone outside your company.	8%	36%	44%	12%
A letter or e-mail, followed by a telephone call.	4%	20%	40%	36%
Cold call by telephone.	0%	20%	36%	44%
Contact at an off-site event.	0%	44%	32%	24%

Interestingly, an overwhelming majority of that 80% would not meet with a salesperson through a telephone call, yet 44% said they would usually meet if they were contacted at an off-site event. When analyzing this data, it becomes clear that in order to meet with many C-level executives, being referred by someone within their organization or meeting them at off-site events like a trade show, tennis court, or perhaps within a social media group is their preference .

Studying or researching your prospect while being prepared and positioned properly is essential for successful selling in the 21ˢᵗ century. Failure to invest the time necessary in preparation will limit your success in front of the customer. The more you build your personal brand and network, the more trust and referrals you will generate. Remember, it should always be your objective to create a pull strategy, because it can be exhausting when you push.

CHAPTER 5 - *The Ask Step (Part 1)*
Personality Type Determines the Questions You Ask

Now that we've invested the time necessary to study the prospective customer's industry, the competitive situation and competitor's territory manager, you are prepared for the meeting to begin. The art of asking effective questions then becomes key.

According to research at the University of Pennsylvania, only 7% of communication is verbal. The tone of our voice constitutes 38%, body language or physiology makes up 55%. More than half of the communication between two people is done through the body. So our facial expressions, mouth, eyes, hands, arm movement, and the use of our legs all speak volumes about us.

Considering the statistics, it is imperative when meeting our prospect for the first time to understand there's a lot more going on than just asking questions. There are two skills you require to better understand your prospect before you sit down and attempt to communicate with him.

The first skill is to understand the different personality types and learn how that knowledge will improve communication.

Four Personality Types

The notion of four distinct personality types may be a new concept to you, but this idea dates back to 370 BC.

Hippocrates, the ancient Greek physician, developed a theory that human emotions and behaviors were the result of body fluids, or humours – blood, yellow bile, black bile, or phlegm.

Western astrology uses the four elements – fire, earth, air and water – in conjunction with the 12 signs of the zodiac. The fire signs are Aries, Leo, and Sagittarius. The air signs are Gemini, Libra and Aquarius. Water signs include Cancer, Scorpio, and Pisces. The earth signs are Taurus, Virgo, and Capricorn. There are many different models of behavior grouping; however, they all have four personality traits associated to them.

In 1921, Swiss psychiatrist and writer Carl Jung published his book on psychological types. It was the first to scientifically document the four functions of consciousness.

He wrote that we have two perceiving functions (sensor and intuition) and two judging functions (thinking and feeling).

The table below is designed to show you the different schools of thought on the four personality types from ancient Greece to the present day. You'll notice only the names change. And this is by no means an exhaustive list.

Personality Type Equivalents Table				
Merrill – Reid	Driver	Expressive	Amiable or Relater	Analytical
D.E.S.A	Dominant	Expressive	Solid	Analytical
Hippocrate	Choleric	Sanguine	Phlegmatic	Melancholy
Western Astrology	Fire	Air	Water	Earth
The P's	Powerful	Popular	Peaceful	Perfect
The S's	Self-Propelled	Spirited	Solid	Systematic
The a's	Administrative	Active	Amiable	Analytical
LEAD Test	Leader	Expresser	Dependable	Analyst
Biblical Characters	Paul	Peter	Abraham	Moses
Animals	Bear	Monkey	Dolphin	Owl
True Colors (1978)	Green	Orange	Blue	Gold

The four personality types are built upon two classes of customer behavior.

Indirect Versus Direct – An indirect person tends to avoid expressing her feelings or thoughts. A direct person tends to utilize her thoughts and feelings to influence or convince others to help her with her plans, goals and expectations.

Open Versus Guarded – An open person tends to make personal relationships his main priority. In more popular terms, an open person is "extroverted." A guarded person tends to focus on the accomplishment of the task or job at hand. He'd be considered "introverted."

The 4 Personality Types – Quadrant

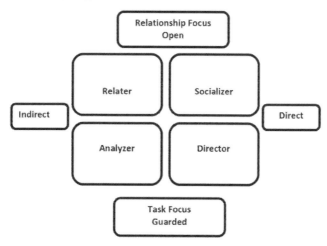

The above diagram provides a great visual for identifying the four styles of relating to the world. Making a determination of what personality describes you and your preferred communication style will allow you to understand your behavior more clearly.

All four personality types see the world in a completely different way. Understanding these differences will allow you to communicate more effectively in both your personal and professional life.

The Socializer / Expresser (Direct and Open)

The socializer is an expressive person who likes to talk and is thought of as assertive and outgoing. He feeds on praise and admiration from others. He openly talks about his dreams and goals for the future and tends to get others involved and committed to their vision. The socializer likes to dress in flashy clothes and is likely to drive an expensive car. This satisfies his need to receive positive acknowledgement from others.

The socializer dislikes conflict with other people and many consider him to be a poor listener. He dislikes routine tasks, line-ups, and rules, and is not detail oriented.

The socializer does not respond well to a director or dictator-type personality. But if he is inspired to accomplish an objective, you may not find a more dedicated and committed person.

Socializers at a Glance

Assertive and responsive
Impulsive, intuitive, spontaneous
Relationship-focused
Emotional and expressive
Short on details
Very persuasive
Talkative
Risk taker
Flashy, sharp dresser
Poor listener
Hates details
Jumps from activity to activity
Works quickly

Craves social interaction
Loves an audience

Suitable careers: The socializer usually will gravitate towards careers that allow use of his persuasive skills. You can find socializers in the field of sales and entertainment. They make excellent social directors or trial attorneys, and they do well in public relations. Entrepreneurship usually satisfies the socializer's need for autonomy and dislike of routine and rules.

The Director (Direct and Guarded)

The director personality is action and goal-oriented, and she needs to see immediate results. These individuals like to lead and take charge of tasks to ensure they will achieve their goals.

The director can be described as a workaholic. She is often the first in the office and the last to leave in the evening. This behavior often finds her neglecting her personal and social lives. Directors are risk takers, and they often bend the rules to achieve their goals. They are likely to gravitate towards high-risk circumstances to experience the thrill of controlling something new.

Directors are known to give gifts of cash, as they rarely take the time to shop for gifts. They're not overly concerned about relationships and focus primarily on their professional performance and how their product or service will impact the bottom line.

Directors at a Glance
Assertive
Task oriented
Decisive and determined
Emotionally guarded
Efficiency focused
Wants control
Impatient
Poor listener
Introverted or guarded
Bottom-line focused
Conservative dresser
Wants the facts
Dislikes feelings or advice

Argumentative
High ego need
Goal oriented

Suitable careers: The director personality will usually gravitate toward careers that allow her to being in control and achieve her goals. You can find director personalities in the fields of executive leadership or authorship. They'll be hard-driving salespeople, coaches, Army generals, and in positions of authority and power. These positions mean they need to be in control and achieve their goals, which explains why the top 5% of all achievers are generally directors/driver personalities.

The Thinker/Analyzer (Indirect and Guarded)

The thinker is generally indirect and task-oriented. They like collecting information and data to assist them in making the correct purchasing decision. A thinker does not like to be wrong or make poor decisions; therefore he pays attention to the details, wanting as much information as possible.

It is wise to ask the thinker what information he would like you to provide. This will prevent you from giving him unwanted features on your product or service.

Thinkers like to be well-informed and will research your company, the competitors, and the manufacturer's specifications. You don't want to get into debates with thinkers. They'll continue to debate or argue until they've won the argument. They are so detailed-oriented that they are usually well-informed with the facts.

The thinker is not overly concerned with style and can be seen in old clothes with a pocket full of pens, with tape keeping his glasses from falling apart.

Thinkers at a Glance

Detail oriented
Like information
Introverted
Analytical
Like product features

Conservative in dress
Ask lots of questions
Need to be correct
Dislike surprises
Thrive in a structured environment
Focus on processes
Loner, works independently
Problem solver
Very loyal
Difficult to change his mind

Suitable careers: The thinker/analyzer will generally gravitate toward careers where he can work independently and nurture his need for data. You can generally find thinkers in careers such as computer programming, accounting, and mathematics.

The Relater (Indirect and Open)

The relater is relationship-oriented and likes to interact with others and work in a team environment. The relater is very intuitive and is focused on people's non-verbal behavior. She tries to ensure harmony and open communication between team members and family, and she works well in a social environment.

Relaters are often some of the best players in any organization. They provide encouragement to their co-workers and will often go beyond the call of duty. They are usually generous givers and great listeners, often exhibiting their kindness to others by listening carefully to a complete stranger. Of the four personality types, the relater is most different from the director. The relater's nature is to avoid conflict and back down or withdraw when tension is apparent. The director is confrontational, task-oriented and shows little regard for feelings or emotions.

Relaters at a Glance

Words motivate them
Strong sense of values
Team player
Likes stability
Supportive
Take things personally
Wants to be popular

Likes references
Avoids risk
Dislikes conflict
Accommodates others
Loves security
Wants to be appreciated
Strong counseling skills

Suitable careers: The relater will usually be in positions that entail creating a connection with other people. Relaters are the teachers, caregivers and counselors of the world.

Adapting To Your Customer

When trying to understand and communicate with the different personality types, it's important to remember that human nature makes us gravitate toward someone who thinks and responds to things as we do. We like people who are like us. This explains why people need to have associations, clubs, and organizations that are filled with people who are like-minded. So it's important to know and understand each of the four personalities and adapt our own communication style when dealing with personality types that are unlike our own.

Know Thyself

For those in the business world or anyone trying to persuade someone to adopt your point of view, it is important to know which personality type you most closely fit. Once you have identified your personality type, you may find that you have been communicating, presenting, or selling in a manner that corresponds to who you are as a person.

If you are a thinker, you may have been selling by providing all the features your product or service has and the cost breakdown in comparison to the competition. There would be little doubt that you were successful selling to other thinkers; however, you may have had great difficulty selling to any of the other three personalities.

Below is a short 20-question survey that's designed to assist you in determining your own personality type.

You may want to circle more than one behavior per question; this is natural. We each exhibit parts of each of the personality types. But the reality is we gravitate toward one behavior type over others. If you have difficulty being objective with yourself, ask someone you know well what they think you would do in response to each question. The intent is to have some fun with the survey and become more aware of the four personality types.

I understand that the responses provided won't always describe you exactly or cover the myriad emotions and reactions that are generated within each of us. When you read each question, ask yourself, "In general, which of these answers usually would apply to me?"

Move through the questions rapidly, trusting in your intuitive response, which is usually the most accurate.

1. I like to help others:
    a. understand facts and details
    b. have fun at what they do
    c. complete what they start
    d. feel good

2. I would rarely say,
    a. "I'll do it right away."
    b. "I'll contemplate this carefully."
    c. "I'll do as you like."
    d. "You are totally wrong."

3. I most want to:
    a. show understanding
    b. enjoy myself
    c. overcome a challenge
    d. form closer relationships

4. I would consider myself to be:
    a. thoughtful and determined
    b. friendly and outgoing
    c. a driver and goal setter
    d. dependable and committed

5. I have difficulty:
    a. working quickly for an extended time

    b. following up on details

    c. having patience with others who procrastinate or show weakness

    d. being assertive

6. I like to give people:
    a. the right information
    b. a smile or laugh
    c. something to challenge them
    d. help when needed

7. I could show you a long list of:
    a. facts about something of interest
    b. those whom I consider friends
    c. my short and long term goals
    d. things I value

8. I do not like:
    a. feeling hurried
    b. to be alone
    c. to admit I lost
    d. to hurt anyone

9. What motivates me is:
    a. the desire to learn and do a job well
    b. new adventures
    c. challenges and crisis intervention
    d. developing close relations

10. I base my decisions on:
    a. careful consideration and reason
    b. emotion and intuition
    c. impulse reactions
    d. how others' feel and my own instinct

11. My friends would consider me:
    a. well-informed and cautious
    b. friendly and a cheerful companion
    c. tough and unafraid
    d. loyal and patient

12. What I fear most is:
    a. confusion and emergencies
    b. not being liked by others

    c. losing command of a situation
    d. conflict

13. I don't like people who:
    a. make me rush
    b. are not interesting
    c. are weak-willed
    d. are unfeeling

14. I am certain that:
    a. I can learn about anything if I try
    b. I can overcome obstacles by influencing with my character
    c. I can master any test or challenge
    d. I value friends and family over monetary success

15. When making a key decision I will:
    a. collect all pertinent facts, consider them, and decide on a careful and logical decision
    b. make an impulsive decision based on feelings at the time, and change my mind later if I want to
    c. arrive at the best possible decision, expecting that others will comply
    d. ask how others would be affected by my behavior, and consider their welfare

16. If I chose one word to describe myself, it would be:
    a. intellectual
    b. sociable
    c. tough
    d. loyal

17. I enjoy:
    a. learning new things
    b. talking to people
    c. being a winner
    d. being giving and caring

18. I prefer to do things:
    a. the right way the first time
    b. by having fun, because I like change and excitement
    c. my way, because I like to control the situation
    d. without a fight, as I dislike conflict with others

19. I prefer people who are:
    a. logical and tolerant
    b. impulsive and vigorous
    c. capable and accommodating
    d. friendly and understanding

20. I like to think that I am:
    a. right
    b. happy and friendly
    c. in control
    d. empathetic

Now add up the number of questions where you circled the letter A, those with letter B, and so on. Write your totals below. The goal is to work towards an equal balance of all four of these personality styles; therefore the closer you are to that already, the better.

A. Analyzer	C. Driver
B. Expresser	C. Relater

Communicating with a Socializer

When communicating with a socializer it is important to be genuinely interested in him and to support him beliefs. Be upbeat and keep the conversation fast-paced while keeping the focus on him. Get everything in writing or summarize what you've agreed upon in an email, because attention to detail is not the socializer's strong point.

Socializers want to know that your product or service will make them look good in front of others. Once you have sold to a socializer, look at all the details – paperwork, training, setup, and maintenance. With a socializer you want to demonstrate how your product can help him achieve their goals. Focus on the big picture.

Communicating with the Director

When communicating with the director, it is important to demonstrate that you understand her goals and her objectives. Don't waste time with making small talk. Get right to the purpose of your call and explain how you can help her get where she want to go. Directors make decisions fast and are task oriented, therefore be quick and well-prepared. Explain what your product does, the time commitment required and the return on investment. Demonstrate how your product or service can help them achieve their goals and objectives.

Communicating with a Relater

When communicating with the relater, be open, honest, and welcoming. Don't get down to business right away.

Make a genuine effort to get to know him, but don't be insincere. The relater is very intuitive and will sense your insincerity immediately. The relater is comfortable discussing his family, friends, hobbies, and personal story. Don't try to rush a relater. Allow him the time to develop trust in you, your product, and your company. Request that he include others in the decision process – he tends to involve others to validate his inclusion within his work environment.

Since relaters like to build long-term relationships, they can become long-term customers for you and even, in some cases, life-long friends.

Communicating with the Thinker

When communicating with the thinker, remember that she is a risk-avoider and change usually involves risk. Like the director, the thinker is task-oriented, so get down to business quickly. Be prepared to provide guarantees that will reduce the risk of making a poor decision: risk free guarantee is one way to gain their trust and business. The thinker loves to look at data, charts and graphs. Detailed information helps the thinker when making a decision.

Since the thinker likes to look at the data and does not want to be embarrassed by making the wrong decision, consider providing her with a competitive analysis of your product versus other industry leaders. Present your product in a systematic way by providing factual information. But don't rush a thinker to a decision. Let her think it over. In the end, 100% of decisions are based on emotion and justified by logic, so give the thinker every reason to believe in you and your product. All things being equal, she will choose you because you have communicated in a language she understands.

Conclusion

As you adapt your communication style to suit those you're interacting with, you improve your effectiveness in communicating feelings and ideas. You'll also improve relationships and avoid miscommunication, which is rampant these days.

Understanding the four personality types is part 1 of the **ASK,** a portion of the S.A.L.E.S. Formula™. Before we ask questions, we need to ensure that we are able to communicate the question in a way that our customer understands.

Part two concentrates on the physiology of our communication (which, if you recall, accounts for 55% of communication). The next step is to utilize the power of body language to make a powerful connection with anyone, anytime.

CHAPTER 6 - *The Ask Step (Part 2)*
Building Rapport

The ability to build rapport with words is strong, however combining words and body language together to create rapport is powerful.

Rapport is the ability to create synergies with another individual, to enter another person's world, to see the world from his or her perspective. And good rapport allows someone else to see the world through your eyes.

All great leaders, politicians, parents, teachers, and salespeople have either consciously or subconsciously worked to create rapport with people in order to influence and persuade action and change.

One of the most effective and impactful ways to create rapport is through what's commonly known in neuro-linguistic programming (or NLP) as mirroring or matching. Mirroring is the art of building rapport through creating physiological similarities with those you're communicating with.

Dr. Milton Erickson, the great hypnotherapist, discovered that by copying or mirroring someone's tone of voice, gestures, and breathing patterns, you can create instant rapport in a matter of minutes. The words we speak may be working on our conscious minds, but the physiological specifics of our body language is working on our subconscious minds – "This person likes me. I trust this person. He's a good person. I'll do business with this guy." This is all done on a subconscious level, and we are typically unaware of anything going on but the relationship being created.

Think of your friends and the people you associate with on a regular basis. Chances are that they have the same interests or beliefs as you do. That's why clubs, associations, and churches are so popular – people don't go to a church or belong to an association with people who believe differently than themselves or interpret Scriptures differently.

People Like People who are Like Them

We are all attracted and drawn to someone who believes and behaves like we do, and we avoid people who don't believe or act like us. When two people are in sync or on the same wavelength, they've created that state of rapport where their beliefs, thoughts, actions, and behaviors are alike.

You have probably experienced this at some point in your life, that feeling of complete alignment with another individual. You feel you've met your soul mate. You laugh together, cry together, and are in a state of complete ecstasy; when he yawns or she yawns, you yawn, and vice versa. This is a subconscious process, and while you shouldn't expect your business relationships to reach this kind of deep level, the same principles can be applied to make those business relationships stronger.

Through the use of mirroring, you can create this rapport or state with anyone at any time by simply matching his or her physiological movements.

How to Mirror

"Mind and body are part of the same system. What occurs in one part will affect all the other parts."
– Sue Knight

So, how do you mirror another person's physiology?

Consider you're the B2B salesperson making a call on a prospective customer for the first time.

You know nothing about this person, except for some preliminary research you've compiled before the meeting. Using this research, you've decided on your customer's personality type, based on the type of position he holds. You can expect your customer will be holding a bit of tension, depending on his past experience with salespeople and whether or not he takes the passive or aggressive position during the meeting.

Once you're invited into his office, you see him sitting behind his desk with his legs crossed and arms folded across his chest, leaning back in his chair. You realize immediately that he is not receptive to you or your message, and he probably believes you're going to try to sell him something he doesn't want or try to change something with which he is quite comfortable.

Everything we have discussed up to this moment has prepared you for the first five seconds of meeting this prospect. The way you prospect, position yourself, dress, your smile, and your general appearance is either confirming or changing the assumptions he has made about you.

The remainder of the communication process will be 7% verbal, 38% tone of voice, and 55% physiology or body language.

Five Second Delay

The way to build and create instant rapport is to mirror, match, or copy the prospect in one or more of the following ways using a five second delay after his actions.

Mirror the way he speaks, including the tone he uses to express his thoughts, the pitch he uses when speaking and the pace he uses to express himself. Does he use big words or short phrases? Use some of the same words he uses (in the proper context, of course!) Mirror his posture, including body movements, speed, eye contact, facial gesture, and hand movement, any and all forms of communication in verbal expression, tone, and physiology.

Remember as a child playing the game Simon Says? It's a game where one person plays Simon. She makes a movement with her body, like crossing her arms or jumping up and down in one place. If she says, "Simon Says," before she makes the movement and you follow her lead, you are still in the game. If she makes a move but does not say "Simon Says" first and you copy her movement, then you are out of the game.

Think of mirroring as playing "Simon Says." If you listen closely and mirror the customer's movement, you will win the game of building rapport. I recommend you practice in private before you perform in public. Make it a game as you meet and interact with people at the grocery store, movie theaters, or a social gathering. Anywhere that people are, you can practice emulating or mirroring their body's facial expressions, tones of voice, or gestures. Watch your own rapport skills increase.

Once you are comfortable mirroring, the next step is to lead them or have them subconsciously mirror you and your movements. This is a powerful and effective method in turning an adversary into an ally, or a foe into a friend.

Leadership is influence, and influence is building rapport with other people so they trust you to lead them into uncharted territory. It's a choice that must be mutually beneficial for all involved, so the stakes are high.

CHAPTER 7 - *The Ask Step (Part 3)*
Always Seek Knowledge

Buyer's Current Status

Organic growth is becoming more and more challenging in today's business climate; the 2008 financial collapse has not made this any easier.

Order takers are no longer able to grow the business or add value to the buyer. In the 21st century, selling is all about adding value to the customer and helping him grow his business while utilizing your product or service. The skills required in selling large accounts are significantly different and **require an effective formula to be successful.**

Studies indicate that when selling a product or service that requires a substantial investment, the final decision is usually coming from the

C-suite. A "product focused" order taker is not able to communicate in the language of the C-level executive, and he cannot strategically position himself as someone who can positively impact their P&L statement or create value for their company.

The 21st Century salesperson is in the business of creating, servicing, and managing demand, while demonstrating to the customer that he has the business acumen to help them achieve or improve their internal and external pressures.

During the questioning process, the buyer is asking himself whether he has a problem and what is the potential impact of that problem. While most order takers are efficient at selling to a buyer who is actively seeking to make a purchase, they usually lack the skills to create value when a buyer is satisfied and content.

Selling to a contented buyer is much more challenging, because no problem exists before your initial call. This is why strong executive selling skills are the differentiators to successful selling in the 21st century.

It is during the asking phase that the seller must identify company goals, then find, grow, and create dissatisfaction. When selling to large accounts, the focus should be establishing a commitment to take the next step in the process since receiving an order is very unlikely at this juncture.

Before you Establish a Meeting

Hypothesis

Before you make contact with the buyer, begin by writing a hypothesis of the issues, problems, or challenges you think your prospect experiences. Based on your experience and the preliminary research you've gathered, ask yourself what problems your product or service solves. What do you need to learn from your prospect before you can be certain that you can make a positive impact on their business? You may have to peel away some layers before you identify their core issues and challenges. But the time you spend will be worth it.

Remember, you're in front of the buyer to create a desire in them for change. You're also hoping to convince them that you are capable of leading them down that path of change. Carefully crafted, thought-provoking questions lead the buyer on a journey to discover that change is necessary.

As an example, beginning your meeting by stating that you reviewed their income statement and noticed that they were behind the industry average by 1% should gain their attention. Connecting metrics and the financial position of their business to that of the industry average will start a conversation that any C-level executive will want to engage in passionately.

Understand that internal and external pressures provide both positive and negative consequences, and executives are looking at these variables each and every day. The primary concern of the executive is to improve the financial position of his organization. Your ability to think beyond the current sales opportunity and look at the executive's business from a 40,000 foot view – while determining how you can assist them with their long-term financial position over the next one, three, or five years – is not something the average competitor is currently providing in the marketplace.

You do not want to ask questions or discuss ideas to which you cannot provide solutions. Therefore begin with your starting hypothesis, see how your client responds, and determine what direction the conversation should take.

Good call planning means creating questions that lead the customer to consider you to be the best answer.

Value of a Value Proposition

A value proposition is the benefit your customers receive by doing business with you; it addresses a specific issue or problem they have that your product or service solves.

Many sellers are unable to articulate a value proposition that differentiates their company, so they're placed into commoditization in the mind of the buyer. There are a few important questions that a value proposition must address.

- In what ways is your product or service innovative and unique?
- How is your product or service a benefit to your target buyer?

- Does your offering create excitement or address the concerns of your target market?
- How are you are different from your competitors?

It's important to tweak your value proposition to fit your target market. A "one size fits all" proposition will not articulate the attributes that matter most to your individual customers.

Having researched your target market, their industry, and their company during the study process, you should have enough information to develop a value proposition that's relevant to your target market.

A Weak Value Proposition

Many value propositions are weak and focus on the features that the seller's product or service has rather than the benefit it provides. Some examples of things to avoid in developing your value proposition:

- ✓ we improve bottlenecks that impede production
- ✓ we specialize in development and education
- ✓ we provide great service and support for customers

The above examples do not describe a benefit or create an image of differentiation or specialization. The examples don't stand out from the millions of competitors in the market. Buyers are inundated with massive amounts of information all the time, and your value proposition must immediately differentiate you and cause the buyer to visualize the benefit that your product will provide them.

Would you be motivated to take action if you received the following voicemail?

"Hello. My name is Adon Rigg, and I am with the Insightful Selling Solutions. We lead the industry in sales training. I'm calling to set up an appointment and introduce you to my company, to see if we can be of value to your organization. I'm in your area next week on Wednesday. Please call me at..."

I think you will agree that the above voicemail does not differentiate the seller or provide any benefit to motivate the buyer to take action. Now compare that to the following:
"Hello. My Name is Adon Rigg. I understand that you recently acquired a few new sales reps. I would like to show you a formula to expedite the

learning curve and improve their success rate from an average of 43% to 96% which is a 223% improvement in as little as 30 days. I'm in your area next week on Wednesday. Please call me at..."

So, what does a strong value proposition look like and how do you create one?

A Strong Value Proposition

A strong value proposition uses terminology that matters to your target buyer, specifically in dollars or percentage terms. Let them know what they can expect to enjoy by doing business with you. The higher these numbers and the nicer these statistics, the more attractive your value proposition will appear.

All buyers and decision makers are responsible for their company's income statement, and therefore your value proposition must address these concerns. A strong value proposition will always address measures that directly or indirectly impact the income statement, and any buyer will be interested to hear the terminology of business: reduce labor costs, decrease employee turnover, reduce operation costs, lower cost of sales, increase market share, reduce cost per customer, increase sales per customer, improve profitability, and improve employee morale.

In today's marketplace most products are a commodity or at risk of becoming one very quickly, therefore the real value proposition is the expertise and insight you provide.

How Do We Create a Value Proposition?

Existing customers are your greatest resource for information and can provide useful insight into what value you provide and how it has impacted their business. Talk to your existing customers about how your product or service has benefited their company. You may be surprised at the answers they give you; this can be extremely important in developing a strong value proposition.

The more information, data, insight, opinions, thoughts, results, feedback, experiences, setbacks, obstacles, and challenges they provide you, the stronger your value proposition will become.

What Questions to Ask

Start by developing a list of questions centered on the benefits your customer experienced using your product or service. Ask them:

- What benefit did my product or service provide you?
- What was the financial impact realized by the product or service?
- How did this improve your internal and external pressures?
- Why was this improvement relevant to your company?
- Did this improve operational costs?
- Did this improve productivity?
- What can you do now that you couldn't do before?
- What does that mean financially to your organization?
- Are there any other areas in your company that benefited from our product service?

This should generate the information needed for developing a strong value proposition.

If you're unable to obtain data from customers, consider using industry statistics to help develop and support your value proposition. In selling sales training, you might quote that 90% of learning is forgotten within three months unless management reinforces the learning. You might also quote that only 4% of sales managers believe their sales team members explore the depth and scope of their customers' issues to reveal challenges they didn't realize they had.

In either case you're citing relevant and pertinent information that can benefit your buyer without providing actual customer feedback.

What is a Value Proposition Statement?

A value proposition is a statement that clearly articulates the real benefit you provide the buyer; it is the primary reason the buyer will decide to meet with you. By following the first step, "study," you should have the insight and information necessary to determine the buyer's needs and values that will impact their business. You can then create a value proposition that speaks directly to your target market, clearly explaining the benefits they will receive by purchasing your product or service.

Your value proposition should be short and easy to remember. It should address common issues or challenges they face. In many situations, these issues have not been identified by the buyer, but they will always be directly or indirectly linked to the income statement. The better your value proposition, the stronger chance you'll have to create opportunities with your buyer.

Here are the five rules to a powerful value proposition:

1. **Attention** – A powerful value proposition gets the attention of the buyer immediately and creates a desire to learn more about you.
2. **Differentiate** – Your value proposition must differentiate you from the competition.
3. **Position** – Your value proposition must position you as someone who can provide insight and value.
4. **Rapport** – If your value proposition gains their attention, differentiates you from others, and positions you properly, it will be easy to build rapport with the buyer. You'll be aligning your abilities with their organizational goals and objectives.
5. **Expedite** – A strong, powerful value proposition will expedite the sales process. When the buyer recognizes the ability to improve and impact profitability, decisions are made quickly.

Your value proposition statement is the catalyst to successful selling in the 21st century. It begins the process of leading the buyer from the status quo to a vision of the future and the benefits that you can provide. Your value proposition must create emotion and give the buyer a vision of what you can bring to their company. It should be brief and not sound overly rehearsed, while differentiating you from your competition. It should answer the question, "Why you?"

A strong value proposition should contain the following:

1. **Brevity**. Your value proposition statement needs to be impactful and create strong visuals in the mind of the buyer in 50 words or less.
2. **Focus**. How does this relate to them and why should they care?
3. **Relatable Language**. Use the appropriate industry jargon or idioms. Words are meaningless unless they are understood. Dumb your value proposition down; imagine that you are telling it to a child. How would you describe it? What words would you use?
4. **Motivation**. What internal and external pressures can you alleviate? How much can you improve or reduce those pressures? Does it motivate them to want to take action?

The easiest way to remember the four elements to a strong value proposition is that it needs to be **a <u>short</u> and <u>distinctive</u> statement in a <u>language</u> that <u>motivates</u> the buyer to take action.**

Your value proposition is very important to positioning you positively in the mind of the buyer. Use your value proposition in everything you do, and make it a critical part of your brand. And your brand should project a professional image that provides insight and value to the customer's business.

We know what makes a strong value proposition. Now, let's look at how to design one.

Designing your Value Proposition

1. The first step is to determine how your target market defines value. What does it look like to them? What is the end result they desire? This is not about you and what value you think your customer wants; what matters is how your customer defines value.

2. Define the challenges your product or service solves.

3. Understand the consequences to the challenges they experience. Learn all the primary and secondary effects of these challenges and how they impact profitability.

4. From your customer's perspective, what is the return on investment and return on effort to make these changes? How does it impact their bottom line?

5. Develop your value proposition.

Prospecting with your Value Proposition

A value proposition is an excellent tool for prospecting. Buyers are always looking for ideas, people, and methods that will improve their profitability or operational processes. The language of business is financial, and your ability to position yourself as someone who can impact the bottom line through a powerful value proposition can get you in the door.

The first step is to develop a phone script that focuses on the internal and external pressures that your product or service solves. Second, figure out how to articulate the value that you can provide the customer. Then, dive in. Do not be threatened or fearful of making contact with them. You are not selling a product, but helping them improve their business. Once you're prepared with an understanding of their industry and their particular organization and you have prepared a strong value proposition, any call reluctance should be minimized.

You're not a salesperson, but an executive with insight. Make the call.

Questioning Skills

> "Questioning skills underpin selling in the 21st century"
> – Adon Rigg

The S.A.L.E.S Formula™ concentrates on the approximate 87.5 % of buyers who are in the contented stage (although this percentage is probably much higher). These buyers do not have active needs and are not aware of any problems within their organization or within their department.

If they are aware of an issue or problem, they perceive the issue as either minor or insolvable, and they are not actively looking to make a purchase.

The S.A.L.E.S Formula™ concentrates on two main objectives:

1. Find, create, and grow dissatisfaction until the pain associated with changing surpasses the pleasure of continuing with the status quo.

2. Utilize your executive skills to obtain the information required for you to assist them in achieving their corporate, regional, or individual goals and objectives.

"Following a selling system provides a 96% success rate compared to just 43% for those that do not follow a formula."
– Bill Brooks

Need-Based Questions are No Longer Enough

The consultative or need-based selling process was created in 1987 when Neil Rackham published his remarkable and industry-leading book, "Spin Selling."

Neil Rackham was sponsored by major Fortune 500 companies for 12 years to research the sales profession. Through over 35,000 sales calls with 10,000 salespeople, he set out to determine:

- Are there special skills that make someone successful in **large** sales?
- In successful sales calls, who does most of the talking: the buyer or the seller?

What he found is that contrary to the profession's conventional wisdom, *buyers* did most of the talking in successful large sales.

The research concluded that the most successful salespeople were those who asked the most questions. Not only were they asking more questions, they were asking smart questions and tended to ask them in a particular sequence.

They began with finding a problem that needed to be fixed. They then associated an implication or consequence of the problem. And then they would have the customer explore what benefits to the organization came from finding a solution. Finally, they would offer a solution; generally a sale was made.

A shift happened because of the seven game changers we discussed in Chapter 1. To refresh your memory, those seven game changers are:

1. Internet
2. Sales 2.0
3. Web 2.0
4. Inflation
5. Best practices
6. Changing demographics

Commoditization

Because of these changes salespeople are becoming less effective, and they now saddle the company with a higher financial burden. The skills that worked in the past now simply place a salesperson into commoditization and a price-centered sale.

The S.A.L.E.S. Formula™ is not about selling solutions to problems because two changes have made this solution selling approach less useful:

1. There's been a shift from the executive as a problem fixer to the executive as the opportunity creator.
2. There's been a shift from selling value communication to selling value creation.[5]

Prior to 20 years ago (when "Spin Selling" came out) growth came from fixing problems, so selling models that focused only on uncovering and developing problems was entirely appropriate. Today, the most dramatic growth opportunities come from divergence with diverse or different offerings. Salespeople following problem-based models often fail to uncover opportunities until very late in the call, if it all.[6]

Making the transition from sales professional to an executive with insight will help you think and converse in the language of senior executives and break-away from the price centered sale.

The S.A.L.E.S Formula™ will help you demonstrate to the buyer your ability to:

1. Relieve the internal and external pressures of their company.
2. Help buyers achieve their short-term or long-term goals and objectives.

In both cases your objective is to positively impact one or more sections of their income statement.

The way to impact a company's income statement is to determine their internal or external pressures and organizational objectives for the next one to five years.

You'd determine those pressures and objectives by asking effective and relevant questions. To do this takes knowledge, financial intelligence, and executive insight.

This focus on the income statement will differentiate you from a salesperson who talks about products, quotes price, and takes orders. You will become an executive who is positioned as a resource to your customers' business operations.

This influential and leadership position will also position you within your own company as someone of value and one whom the company will strive to keep satisfied. It could also make you one of the highest-paid sales professionals in your industry.

Questions are Answers

Always arrive at your meeting with an in-depth understanding of your prospect's business and their industry. Use this information to create a list of questions that are designed to provoke, challenge, and engage the customer. Then you can establish in their mind the need for change.

The questions you ask should encourage your prospect to think outside the box on the responses, beliefs, and opinions they hold. You are asking questions to influence the customer's thinking, so be careful that you don't cross-examine or interrogate him. Establish a respectful and professional relationship while learning what you need to know.

Types of Questions

First ask **operational** questions about their company – these answers you can't get anywhere else. Then, concentrate on areas and subjects you have confidence in, areas that your product or service can positively impact.

- ✓ Never ask an operational question that you can get from another source such as the Internet.
- ✓ Ask open-ended questions that entice the customer to explain how they feel, how they think, what they want, what they see, what they believe is possible.
- ✓ Ask questions that help you identify the processes, procedures, history, and existing situation of the company.

- ✓ Ask questions to assist you in determining their desires, thoughts, and feelings, to determine their purchasing motivation.
- ✓ Ask questions that are thought-provoking, well-meaning, and empathetic, but not inappropriate or overtly personal.

- ✓ Ask questions in layman terms. Do not put the customer in a position to feel inferior, incompetent, or unintelligent.
- ✓ Ask questions in a systematic way. Avoid asking questions that take your prospect from topic to topic. Stay focused.
- ✓ When the customer responds to a question, ask another question that leads your prospect to expand deeper on the topic.
- ✓ Ask follow-up questions like: "How do you mean exactly? Could you elaborate? What was the effect of that decision? Is there anything else?"

Once you have your list of questions you need to be more precise and methodical in preparation for your meeting.

Here are some things to consider:

- ✓ Questions need to center around the internal and external pressures of their business. That is the purpose of your call.
- ✓ Questions need to guide the customer to the conclusion that you intend.
- ✓ Questions must uncover and expose the negative aspects of their current situation.
- ✓ Questions must be relevant and thought-provoking.
- ✓ Questions need to capture the language that creates the desire to take action.
- ✓ Questions need to create an atmosphere that inspires ideas, solutions, and possibilities.
- ✓ Questions must be relevant to the buyer and their company.
- ✓ Questions cannot be evasive or disrespectful.
- ✓ Questions must move you towards a desired outcome.
- ✓ Questions need to make the customer think of the problem or solution that you want them to think about.
- ✓ Many prospects are reluctant to share or divulge information, particularly during the early stages of the initial sales call.
- ✓ Average questions receive average information.
- ✓ Thought-provoking questions receive thought-provoking answers.

✓ Good questions move the selling process forward at a steady but unpressured pace; this makes landing the sale easier. [7]

✓ Before responding to a question, pause for a moment and determine why they may be asking you that particular question.

Questions are the executive's greatest resource.

Who, What, When, Where, Why, and How

Using Who, What, Where, When, Why, and How questions is an excellent way to obtain information from the customer. They don't allow for quick "yes" or "no" responses. They make the customer expand upon a topic and provide a detailed answer to the questions you ask.

- What differentiates you from your competitor?
- What demographic is your main customer? Who are they?
- Who is your target market?
- What need does your product or service fill?
- What are your departmental goals in the coming year?
- What are the company goals for the next one or two or three years?
- How many suppliers do you presently use?
- How do you measure supplier capabilities?
- What is the biggest challenge in your business?

After each question, follow it up immediately with a question that penetrates further and deeper into the topic. The following are excellent follow-up questions.

- How do you mean?
- Can you expand on that?
- Can you tell me how?
- How does that affect…?

Questions open the lock to creating new customers, **if** you are prepared properly. Asking effective questions obtains information which you can then apply to impact the customer's income statement. Asking questions with clarity and effectiveness, while leading the customer through a systematic and logical approach, will demonstrate to them that you are not an order taker. You are an executive that brings insight and value.

- ✓ Effective questions have the ability to influence and direct the buyer's thinking.
- ✓ Effective questions position you as an expert in the mind of the customer.
- ✓ Effective questions utilize the language that motivates the action and thought process the salesperson intends to create.
- ✓ Effective questions build rapport and allow you to ask clearer and more precise questions.
- ✓ Effective questions and the words you use direct your customer's thought process.
- ✓ Effective questions are designed to peel away the outer layers of a problem to get to its core.
- ✓ Effective questions cause the customer to think of their business in a deeper and more profound way.

The more focused and thought-provoking your questions are, the more your customer must concentrate 100% of their attention on answering them.

Preparation

Before you make your first face-to-face call, it's important to do comprehensive planning and show up prepared.

The following are a few things to be conscious of before you attend that first meeting.

- ✓ Confirm the appointment with both a phone call and an email People are busy and mistakes are made. It's your responsibility to ensure that your prospect knows you're coming. Document it with both a phone call – even if it goes to voicemail – and an email.
- ✓ Have all the information and literature you need with you. There is no excuse to not be prepared. Consider bringing a personalized presentation with printed copies of information you're presenting and want them to remember and review at a later time.
- ✓ Arrive at least 10 minutes early. This will give you time to notify reception of your arrival and allow you to relax both physically and mentally before your meeting.

✓ Are you dressed appropriately for the industry you are calling on? You do not want to overdress or underdress. This could make your contact feel uncomfortable.

Remember, you're always positioning yourself with everything you do.

First Meeting

When meeting with a buyer for the first time, there are a few questions you should address during the initial minutes of the call.

- What business are you in?
- What does your company offer?
- Who are your customers?
- Why are you there?

At the initial meeting, establish your reason for being there. Let them know who your company has worked with in the past and how you helped them achieve results (value proposition). It's important that you position yourself as someone who can provide value to their company and create a collaborative relationship. If you don't, you'll be seen as a price-quoting transactional supplier.

Creating a collaborative relationship begins with demonstrating that you possess insight and expertise that won't come from another supplier. Show them that your insight into their industry is a perspective they won't get from magazines or individual research. This can be the foundation of a long-term business relationship.

Research shows that lately C-level executives are getting involved early in the buying decision. This is where they set the objectives and determine the strategy to move forward, while getting involved again later during the implementation stage. Salespeople who want to escape a transactional sale will need to meet and interact with C-level executives at this stage, before objectives have been established. This requires a salesperson to think, talk, and engage with the senior executive in the language of business.

Meetings with executives are an excellent place to discuss ideas, and salespeople who ask relevant and impactful questions create an atmosphere that's conducive to exploring those ideas. The prepared salesperson can penetrate beyond the surface to expose their problems and challenges.

The meeting should be focused on uncovering problems, examining organizational objectives and exploring the consequences or concerns associated with your findings. The meeting should be centered on asking questions and listening to what is being said. Allow the buyer to express and discover, through your questions, the problems within their company.

The insightful executive takes charge of the meeting, establishing the agenda and setting the expectations and anticipated benefit of the meeting. The average meeting is from 45 to 60 minutes long and should begin with an introduction of your experience. Make sure you follow with your value proposition statement and the value you expect the meeting to deliver.

What the Buyer is Looking For

Buyers reward the seller who creates value for their company. Buyers particularly like sellers who do this and reward them through developing collaborative relationships and not shopping at the competitors.

But when the buyer establishes the need without the assistance of the seller, they will shop the competition. A transactional purchase is inevitable. This demonstrates the power of creating buyer demand and building collaborative relationships. Collaborative relationships are the differentiator for successful selling in the 21st century.

Buyers are willing to pay a premium for expert advice that brings value to their business. The customer is paying for your insight and advice. The product that you supply them is secondary.

You create value and build collaborative relationships with buyers by helping them in one of the following ways:

1. Identify internal and external inefficiencies.
2. Assist them in achieving or meeting organizational goals and objectives.
3. Reveal new revenue-generating opportunities, such as entering new market sectors, or differentiating them to achieve growth within existing markets.

Customers will invest time and resources in those who immediately provide value and impact their business. The sales professional must be proficient and excel within the four executive skill sets. Credibility comes from demonstrating to the buyer that you understand their business and can positively contribute to the bottom line.

Questions are the easiest and most effective way to help the buyer think about their business in a different light. Effective questioning skills allow the buyer to draw their own conclusions, rather than having an outsider telling them they have a problem. Your questions enlighten the buyer to a better way. **People are more inclined to value and invest in something that they have asked for, rather than in something that you have freely offered to them.**

The 21st century professional must utilize their skills and look at their customer's business from a 40,000-foot view. If you do this, you are more likely to develop collaborative relationships with the buyer and enter their inner circle.

You'll know you have achieved this when you are trusted with confidential information and treated as an advisor and consultant.

CHAPTER 8 – THE LEARN STEP
Learn How You Can Impact their Income Statement

Asking questions to learn how you can impact your prospect's income statement is the third step in the five steps of the S.A.L.E.S. Formula™.

When you ask questions, you learn about the customer's business. Then you can contribute by providing insights to impact profitability. The S.A.L.E.S. Formula™ provides a method to understand the buyer's objectives, and it creates an opportunity for the buyer to ask you for your insight on how they can improve their business.

This is your primary objective, and this can only be achieved through asking questions that pertain to the five categories on the income statement.

In order to create change and differentiate yourself, you will have to speak their language. That common business language is finance. Your ability to use this language is what will separate you from your competition and position you as an executive who communicates efficiently and brings value and expertise.

What is Strategy?

Before we address the function of the income statement, we first need to understand strategy. This is the foundation to the success of any company. Strategy is how an organization competes; this determines their competitive advantage in the industry. Every C-level executive is concerned about meeting strategic objectives, as these will always impact profitability and the P&L statement.

An organization's strategic objectives often have three areas of concentration:

1. Corporate
2. Competitive
3. Operational

Corporate Strategy

Corporate strategy concerns the organization's overall value in conjunction with their financial and operational objectives. It centers on fundamental questions like "Why are we in business?" and "Why are we in this particular business?" An organization or corporation must be able to answer these questions in order to provide a vision for the future that has value or meaning. The answer to these questions determines how resources will be dispersed and where they will be invested and divested.

Competitive Strategy

Competitive strategy concerns an organization's current position within their industry and how the company competes in comparison to its competitors. For example, a beauty consultant may differentiate herself by providing house calls if she determines she cannot compete on price with major brick and mortar competitors.

Operational Strategy

Operational strategy concerns financial, research, and strategies or plans of action to strengthen an organization's functional and organizational resources. Typically, these expand into marketing, production, HR and other areas in order to develop core competencies to build a sustainable competitive advantage.

Our job is to determine how we can create value for our customers by helping them achieve their corporate, competitive, or operational strategies, and how we can provide them with a competitive advantage.

Developing a Competitive Advantage

To develop a competitive advantage, the organization needs to differentiate itself from the competition by creating greater customer value in an effort to gain market share. There are three categories for creating a competitive advantage:

1. Cost advantage
2. Product differentiation
3. Transaction advantage

Cost Advantage

Cost efficiencies can provide an advantage over the competition. By manufacturing a similar product at a lower cost than their competitors, a company can gain higher profit margins while still being price competitive. The following are a few areas that can provide a cost advantage.

- ✓ Working at higher levels of productivity can provide reductions in unit costs.

- ✓ Producing a variety of products at a lower cost than another company could produce just one product.

- ✓ New technology and innovation can provide a cost advantage over the competition by implementing new and stronger efficiencies to purge costs within the development process.

Product Differentiation

Product differentiation is manufacturing a product that is unique in the marketplace. This produces higher margins, and customers are generally willing to pay a higher price for enhanced features and benefits that provide a distinguishable advantage.

There are 3 basic categories for product positioning:

1. Genuine product is a product completely new to the market. There is presently nothing like it in the market. This advantage usually does not last longer than a few weeks or months, before the competition emulates something similar. Think the iPad or the Kindle.

2. Commodity is a product that has no differentiator in the marketplace and is generally thought to be exactly like or similar to the competition. The end result of this product category is price. Think toilet paper or bottled water.

3. Brand – If you are not a commodity, you must be a brand. A brand is a product that provides the same benefit as the competitors; however, the customer is willing to pay a higher price to be associated with your product. Think certain cars and designer clothes.

Transaction Advantage

A company has an advantage when they earn greater profits. This can happen in a variety of ways: through innovative transactional processes, by reducing costs, or by making it easier, faster, and more convenient for the customer to purchase.

An example of a transaction advantage is "do it yourself" checkout stands at the grocery store. This reduces the time the customer spends in line to make a purchase. Another example is templates design, which is specific for the customer and allows fast and convenient purchases on regularly-used products on the company website.

A competitive strategy is the "actions and plans" a company uses to counteract the anticipated movement of the competition. It is an essential element of the organization's general strategy that determines how they go to market. Are they a "best price" company? Are they a "best value" company? Are they a leader in innovation? Competitive strategy identifies the company details in pricing, products, and technology that provide the greatest opportunity to beat the competition.

Many companies have found they cannot be all things to all people. They choose the market segments they want to lead, and forfeit others to the competition. This is part of an effective and efficient strategy which allows for a concentration of focus and resource allocation.

Purging costs and maximizing efficiencies are part of an executive team's strategy, and outsourcing can be an effective strategy in meeting these objectives. Functional tasks like finance, human resources, R&D, purchasing, sales, operations, marketing, and information systems can be outsourced. The determining factor of this decision is usually transaction costs, such as the cost of producing that good or service inside the company, while considering both direct and indirect costs of expanding organization responsibilities.

When asking questions of an executive, you should understand and be comfortable discussing their "go to market" strategy and their relative standing in the market. What is their competitive advantage? Are there internal or external factors they have not identified? Are they lacking the resources necessary to strengthen their competitive standing?

The bottom line is that every serious business has a strategy to increase revenue and decrease expenses, while improving profitability. The income statement was created to measure these metrics.

The 21st century executive does not sell product. The 21st century executive provides insightful perspectives and solutions to improve his client's business. They ease internal and external pressures that impact the P&L. They improve profitability. They contribute to the bottom line.

Financial Statements – The Language of Business

Different names for an Income Statement

The income statement provides a snapshot of the financial viability of a corporation, while providing an outlook on the revenue they can generate. The income statement measures the money in (revenue) and the money out (expenses) for a company during a period of time – usually quarterly, but it can be monthly or yearly.

There are many different names for the income statement: profit and loss statement, P&L statement, statement of operations, operating statement, statement of earnings, and earnings statement. Regardless of the name, the format and structure remain the same.

Every employee within an organization contributes to the income statement by either generating profit or creating an expense. The sales manager needs to determine the profits that the sales team is producing for the organization, while the marketing manager must determine which products produce the highest margin for promotional purposes. The office supplies purchaser needs to be aware of how the company spends in relation to their budget and needs to monitor and maintain expenditures.

Sales Inc Income Statement Year Ended December 31st 20XX		
Revenue		**$1,000,000**
Sales		
Subtract: Sales and return allowances	$30,000	
Sales Discounts(Cash Discounts)	10,000	40,000
Net Sales		960,000
Cost of Goods sold		**460,000**
Gross Profit		**500,000**
Selling Expenses:		
Sales Salaries	$125,000	
Advertising	50,000	
Delivery Expense	9,000	
Bad Debt Expense	3,000	
Credit Card Fees	2,500	
Total Selling Expense	189,500	
Administrative Expenses:		
Administrative Salaries	75,000	
Rent	50,000	
Employee Benefits	20,000	
Payroll Taxes	15,000	
Insurance	10,000	
Utilities	3,000	
Office Supplies	4,000	
Depreciation	10,000	
Total Administrative Expense	187,000	
Total Selling& Admin Expense		**376,500**
Net operating Income		123,500
Other income; Interest Income		22,300
Income before Interest and Income Taxes		145,800
Other Expense; interest Expense		12,000
Net Income before Income Tax		133,800
Subtract; Income Tax		32,000
Net Income		**$101,800**

The 5 Main Categories on the Income Statement

Revenue (Sales)

Sales, or revenue, is positioned at the top of the statement and is what is referred to when someone says "top line sales." "Top line sales" means revenue or sales growth and consists of the total dollar value for all products or services a company provides to the customer for a specific period of time.

To be "true revenue," a company must have completed shipment of the product. A service company must have completed the service.

Cost of Goods Sold or Cost of Services

Directly below revenue is cost, commonly known as "cost of goods sold" (COGS) or "cost of services" (COS), depending on whether a product or service is involved.

Cost measures all costs directly involved in producing the product or delivering the service, including materials or labor. This includes the salaries of the employees on the production line and the materials involved to produce the goods. There are gray areas, such as sales commissions and wages for the plant supervisor; however, that is over and above the purpose of this chapter.

Cost of service (COS) for a service company generally includes labor associated with delivering the service.

Gross Profit

Gross profit is measured as such:

Revenue	$1000
Cost of goods sold	$ 600
Gross profit	$ 400

Gross Profit is simply the profit after subtracting cost, but it does not include the operating expenses for the organization.

Operating Expenses

When an expense is not directly involved in production of goods or the performance of a service, it is removed from cost and placed in operating expenses.

Operating expenses (or overhead) include anything needed to operate a business: rent, utilities, telephone, research, marketing, management, HR, and accounting salaries. If the category is not involved with the cost of goods sold or cost of services, then it goes into operating expenses.

Think for a moment of **yourself as a company** that performs labor for your current employer. The labor that you provide is your own personal cost of service, and once you receive your paycheck, all the expenses you pay every month are your own personal operating expenses. This included your mortgage, gas, insurance, food, and entertainment. Whatever is left in the bank is your net profit

Operating Profit, or EBIT

Gross Profit – Operating Expenses = Operating Profit or (EBIT)

Operating profit is also known as EBIT (earnings before interest and taxes). Interest and taxes, at this juncture, have not been subtracted from revenue. The reason for this is that operating profit reveals the true profit the business is able to generate. Taxes have nothing to do with the successful operation of a business.

Operating profit, or EBIT, provides an excellent snapshot of how good an organization is being managed and is watch closely by all interested parties of an organization. It measures the demand for these products or services and the company's efficiency in delivering those products or services. It provides the information that lenders and vendors are interested in, because it reveals the ability of the company to repay loans or pay bills.

Net Profit (Bottom Line)

Net profit is the last line on the income statement. After all expenses are subtracted from revenue, including cost, operating expenses, taxes, interest, one-time charges, and non-cash expenses like depreciation and amortization, the net profit can be determined.

When a company is experiencing net profits that are lower than they should be, there are only three areas to concentrate on that can improve this issue:

1. Increase Sales.
2. Reduce Cost.
3. Reduce Operating Expenses (usually by downsizing employee numbers).

Now that we have discussed the categories of the income statement, we need to look at the pressures directly impacting an organization's profitability. This is where you can provide some insight to buyers on how to improve or alleviate these concerns. If you have followed the S.A.L.E.S. Formula™ in proper formation, then you will <u>have already studied their industry</u>, and you'll be prepared with a hypothesis on how you can add value to their business.

Your objective is to **learn** or confirm what you already know to be common issues within their industry. At this juncture you only want to ask questions that **inspire** your prospect to identify areas within the organization that need improvement.

Your questioning skills should be designed to:

1. Identify internal and external inefficiencies.
2. Identify opportunities to help them achieve and meet organizational goals and objectives.
3. Identify new revenue-generating opportunities, such as entering new market sectors, or differentiating them to achieve growth within existing markets.

In conjunction with our working knowledge of the income statement, we can begin focusing on the indirect and direct pressures which contribute to the profitability of the company.

Three Areas of Focus when Questioning the Customer

There are three types of questions when meeting with a customer. Some you'll use sparingly, others you'll use throughout your conversation, and there will be times you go from one type of question to the next during the questioning process.

✓ External pressures – These questions are about gathering information that you cannot obtain through other sources such as the Internet. You may need to ask questions about customers, suppliers, competition, regulatory issues, and globalization.

✓ Internal pressures – These questions are more specific to the buyer's processes and are designed to uncover problems, concerns, or dissatisfaction within the company or a department. These questions are designed to probe and penetrate beneath the surface in an effort to uncover operational and financial areas of concern. These can be profits, operations, employees, processes, productivity, and company culture.

✓ Goals or Objectives – These questions move you beyond the find, grow, and measure customer dissatisfaction and allow you to determine the organization's strategic objectives .

Corporate or Organization Goals

Corporate or organizational objectives are the large goals which come directly from the top, from the board of directors or the CEO. This is basically the vision the company has for the next one to five years of operation. These goals might include reducing costs, expanding through acquisitions, outsourcing, divesting, and improving net profit by 3% per year.

Regional Goals

Regional goals are set by each department or region head, who generally reports to the CEO or someone at the C-level position. These goals will generally contribute in some way to the company's organizational goals; however, each department head usually has some autonomy in making the changes necessary to accomplish his department's annual goals and objectives.

Individual Goals

Learning the personal goals of the individual you're meeting with and where he sees himself within the company or industry during the next five years can be very beneficial. It will help you to understand what motivates him and how you can position yourself and your company to assist him in achieving these goals.

Examples of goal questions are:

- Where do you see your company three years from now?
- What are your departmental goals or objectives over the course of this year?
- What obstacles are preventing you from achieving your goals today?

Goal questions help the seller understand where the buyer wants to go and how they plan to get there. There are two main strategies behind asking and determining the goals or objectives of the company:

- ✓ To identify and create avenues of alignment with buyers and the goals or objectives.
- ✓ To identify gaps of accomplishment that will represent a starting point to look for dissatisfaction and problems.[8]

Internal Pressures (Drivers)

Internal pressures are the inner workings of an organization that makes the company viable and efficient. These pressures drive revenue, impact profits, and are either financial or operational in nature. Drivers can be anything that management invests time, money, or resources into improving. Profits, costs, operations, talent, productivity, metrics, and culture are examples of areas that your prospect is examining to purge expenses and maximize revenue. Every industry will have different variables, but some of these internal pressures are universal.

Value Chain

Interlinked value-adding activities convert inputs into outputs which, in turn, add to the bottom line and help create a competitive advantage.

A value chain typically consists of:

1) Inbound distribution or logistics
2) Manufacturing operations
3) Outbound distribution or logistics
4) Marketing and selling
5) After-sales service

These activities are supported by:

6) Purchasing or procurement
7) Research and development
8) Human resource development, and
9) Corporate infrastructure.[9]

Financial Pressures (Revenue, Profits, Sales)

All executives are concerned with the financial performance of their organizations, and at the forefront of their minds is cash inflows verse outflows. Insightful selling in the 21st century demands the utilization of the four executive skills while identifying the key business drivers that are specific to their business. Your aim is to position your product or service as something that will improve the company's ability to be better, faster, or simpler than they are presently. Your success will be determined by your ability to improve profit, costs, or expenses of the organization.

For example, an executive for a distribution company will experience internal pressures to improve organic growth, costs of goods sold, profit margins, product rationalization, inventory turns, to reduce accounts receivable, reduce taxes payable, cost per customer, to increase customer retention, employee retention, and to improve competitive positioning. All of the above examples can contribute positively or negatively to the company's bottom line.

Internal Operational Pressures

Executives are always looking to improve internal organization and the effect these improvements have on the financial viability of the organization. The operational pressures or drivers that impact an organization will vary from industry to industry. They can include improving the lead conversion time, employee turnover, talent, productivity, energy consumption, culture, defect reduction, procurement, technology, health and safety, waste reduction, absenteeism, and product quality.

Achieving operational excellence is critical to an organization's sustainability in the marketplace. Minimizing or eliminating these operational pressures positions a company to realize lower costs and deliver superior manufactured goods.

Cost of Goods

We know that cost measures all expenditures directly involved with producing the product or delivering the service including materials or labor. How can your product or service reduce or eliminate these costs? Labor is an expense that many organizations look to reduce. Therefore, if your product or service can reduce the head count needed to produce the client's product or service, then you are directly impacting profits. The question is, "Can your product or service improve production and reduce the time needed to complete the task?"

As an example, in the cleaning industry, the labor involved with vacuuming a conference room using a 36" power head instead of a 12" power head means a 300% improvement in production. This results in less labor time to perform the service or offers the ability to reallocate that labor to additional contracts. Either way the customer decides to look at it, the bottom-line is being positively impacted.

Research and Development

While it differs from industry to industry, the amount of money spent on research and development each year can be in the millions or billions of dollars. Some organizations are dependent on innovation to provide a competitive advantage and increased market share.

Innovation in today's environment can provide an advantage in the competitive marketplace. Maintaining costs within research and development is very difficult because researchers do not know in advance how to achieve the preferred outcome. Therefore, higher research and development investment does not guarantee "greater innovation, greater profits, or increased market share."

For some companies, research and development is a necessity to compete in a highly competitive environment. However, considering the rising costs of labor, regulatory compliance, and materials, there may be opportunities to outsource the research and development department or to reduce costs associated within certain sectors such as private labelling.

Can you provide more value towards this challenge than your competitor can?

Talent

Steve Tappin and Andrew Cave authored the 2008 book titled "The Secrets of CEOs", 150 Global Chief Executives Lift the Lid on Business, Life and Leadership". What they found was that the global war for talent among UK executives was the number one priority for 68% of the CEOs surveyed; comparatively, strategy placed a mere 9% and execution only 25%. According to a Forbes 2007 survey, consisting of a sample of 600 US CEOs, 74% of them consider staffing and human capital issues to be a **very** significant challenge for the company in years ahead.[10]

"CEOs are clear that talent is front of mind. Even those who did not tell us that talent was their number one priority put it in their top three. [12] If you have the right people running the business units, it works magically. It's like turning up the volume."[11]

The First World War for talent will be a central battleground for businesses because it's the result of powerful global demographic forces that will persist far beyond the next decade. Global operations leave business prey to four critical forces: poor Western demographics, the skills shortage in the East, the lack of global leaders, and the frequency with which employees are now shifting jobs.[12]

An executive selling in the 21st century can differentiate himself by providing insight and value to an organization by alleviating some of these pressures.

Can you provide more value towards this challenge than your competitor can?

Turnover

According to People Link Consulting, many employers underestimate the cost of employee turnover. Researchers have estimated the cost of employee turnover as anywhere from 30% to 150% of an employee's annual compensation.

Understand these internal pressures, and reduce or eliminate the cost associated to them.
Consider a company with 100 employees that experiences a turnover rate of 5% per year, with an average yearly salary of $50,000. This turnover rate is potentially costing the organization $75,000 to $375,000 in direct and indirect costs. Reducing this turnover rate by even 1% can provide the company with up to $75,000 in additional profits.

It's clear that in today's ultra-competitive market where product differentiation is becoming more difficult, acquiring and retaining the most talented people is a big concern for today's CEOs. Your ability to position yourself and your product or service to alleviate this concern provides a potential opportunity.

Can you provide more value towards this challenge than your competitor can?

Sales and Marketing

According to Peter Drucker: "People are simply too expensive to be used for selling. We cannot, by and large, sell anymore – we must market, i.e., we must create the desire to buy which we can then satisfy without a great deal of selling."[13]

Peter Drucker has been widely quoted with the following insight:

"Marketing and innovation make money. Everything else in a business is a cost." In other words, product development, marketing, and sales (a subset of marketing) are the drivers of revenue and profit. Everything else is the profit-killing drain on a profit-motivated organization. [14]

Considering that sales and marketing are the lifeblood of an organization and one of only two contributors to driving revenue, how can you contribute to the sales and marketing of your customer's organization? Utilizing the tools of your product, service and experience, how can you create value for their company? Can you help them identify new market segments? Can you assist them with entering these new markets? Can you assist them in differentiating their company? Can you assist them and driving new revenue either through improved sales or marketing practices?

Can you provide more value towards this challenge than your competitor can?

Wikipedia defines Marketing as the process by which companies create customer interest in goods or services. It generates the strategy that underlies sales techniques, business communication, and business development. It is an integrated process through which companies build strong customer relationships and create value for their customers and for themselves. Marketing is used to identify the customer, to satisfy the customer, and to keep the customer.

Processes and Procedures

A Process is a progression of interdependent procedures which, at every stage, consume one or more resources (employee time, energy, machines, or money) to convert inputs (data, material, parts, etc.) into outputs. These outputs then serve as inputs for the next stage until a known goal or end result is reached. [15]

Input
Our resources such as people, raw materials, energy, information, and finance that are put into a system (such as an economy, manufacturing plant, computer system) to obtain desired output(s). Inputs are classified under 'costs' in accounting. [16]

Output
Amount of energy, work, goods or services, etc. produced by a

machine, factory, firm, or an individual in a period. [17]

Procedure

Is a step-by-step sequence of activities or course of action (with definite start and end points) that must be followed in the same order to correctly perform a task. Repetitive procedures are called routines. [18]

Your ability to recognize inefficient and ineffective practices will position you as an expert. Your ability to utilize your product or service and improve their processes and procedures to reduce expenses or increase revenue will cement you as an executive with insight.

Can you provide more value towards this challenge than your competitor can?

Organizational Culture

Is the sum total of an organization's past and current assumptions, experiences, philosophy, and values that hold it together, and are expressed in its self-image, inner workings, interactions with the outside world, and future expectations. It is based on shared attitudes, beliefs, customs, express or implied contracts, and written and unwritten rules that the organization develops over time and that have worked well enough to be considered valid. [19]

Your ability to build or improve the organizational culture to meet the vision that management has can provide long-term benefits to the success of the company and the CEO, while positioning you as an executive that provides and creates value.

Can you provide more value towards this challenge than your competitor can?

Health and Safety

This includes organized efforts and procedures for identifying workplace hazards and reducing accidents and exposure to harmful situations and substances. It also includes training of personnel in accident prevention, accident response, emergency preparedness, and use of protective clothing and equipment. [20]

Your ability to build or improve the health and safety of the employees is of great importance to any respectable organization. The financial consequence to a company because of an injured employee is extensive both from a downtime perspective, as well as from a liability and insurance premium standpoint.

How can your product or service contribute to a safer and healthier work environment?

Can you provide more value towards this challenge than your competitor can?

Management Systems

This includes documented and tested step-by-step methods aimed at smooth functioning through standard practices. Used primarily in the franchising industry, management systems generally include detailed information on topics such as:

1. Organizing an enterprise.
2. Setting and implementing corporate policies.
3. Establishing accounting, monitoring, and quality control procedures.
4. Choosing and training employees.
5. Choosing suppliers and getting best value from them.
6. Marketing and distribution. [21]

Your ability to analyze, evaluate and recommend improvements of organizational systems and the managerial infrastructure can eliminate inefficiencies and increase productivity. This reduces expenses and improves output, which can directly impact the bottom line.

How can your product or service make a positive contribution to the infrastructure of your prospect's business?

Can you position yourself as someone who is an essential resource in assisting with the successful implementation of systems which will improve the infrastructure of the company?

Can you provide more value towards this challenge than your competitor can?

Technology

Technology includes the purposeful application of information in the design, production, and utilization of goods and services, and in the organization of human activities. Technology is generally divided into five categories

1. Tangible: blueprints, models, operating manuals, prototypes.
2. Intangible: consultancy, problem solving, and training methods.
3. High: entirely or almost entirely automated and 'intelligent' technology which manipulates ever finer matter and ever more powerful forces.
4. Intermediate: semi-automated 'partially intelligent' technology that manipulates refined matter and medium level forces.
5. Low: labor intensive 'dumb' technology that manipulates only coarse or gross matter and weaker forces. [22]

Your organization's ability to develop new technology is something that you may have little control over. But it is important to remember that new means "new to your customer," not necessarily new to you. Often a product in your current portfolio, positioned and implemented utilizing new processes, can be equal in benefit to your customer as an entirely new technology.

What existing products and services do you presently have that can be positioned as innovative technology? How can they impact your customer's revenue, cost of goods, margin, expenses, or profitability?

Can you provide more value towards this challenge than your competitor can?

External Pressures

Your objective is to assist your customer in meeting their organizational goals and improving the operational pressures that impact their business internally or externally. The internal pressures are easier for your customer to control, because the sources of these pressures usually originate within the organization.

External pressures are more challenging to control, because they are not as easy to identify and are beyond the control of the company. These pressures can critically impact the organization, and they can come from many different areas such as the economy, new technology, competitors, customers, partnerships, globalization, regulatory issues, and trends such as sustainability.

Identifying external pressures allows an organization to achieve a competitive advantage; your ability to identify these pressures and present a solution to your customer provides a real benefit to their organization. The industry insights you provide have the potential to strengthen their organizational strategy, increase market share, and improve their positioning within the industry. The value you provide may at times be immeasurable in terms of real dollars; however, your ability to provide insight that strengthens their business will not go unnoticed.

It will position you as someone invaluable to their organization.

Supply Chain

In an effort to identify the external pressures that impact your customer's industry, review or study their supply chain. Identify possible bottlenecks, roadblocks and organizational procedures that are potentially impacting their competitive advantage and the bottom line.

A supply chain is a network of entities directly or indirectly interlinked and interdependent while serving the same consumer or customer. It consists of vendors who supply raw material, producers who convert the material into products, warehouses that store, distribution centers that deliver to the retailers, and retailers who bring the product to the ultimate user. Supply chains underlie value-chains because, without them, no producer has the ability to give customers what they want, when and where they want it, at the price they want. Producers compete with each other only through their supply chains, and no degree of improvement at the producer's end can make up for the deficiencies in a supply chain which reduce the producer's ability to compete. [23]

Supplier Pressures

Suppliers play a critical role in supply chain management. With systems like Six Sigma and Total Quality Management, the number of suppliers, particularly for large companies, is constantly being reduced. This is a benefit to the company as it minimizes complexity, provides superior purchasing discounts, and minimizes accounting costs. There are two primary pressures:

1. General: External entity that supplies relatively common, off the shelf, or standard goods or services, as opposed to a contractor or subcontractor who commonly adds specialized input to deliverables.

2. Quality control: Internal or external entity that provides input to jobs or tasks of an organization's internal customers. Efficient interactive relationship between a supplier and a customer is a critical component of quality management. [24]

With these measures in place, there are variables that can negatively impact the supply chain system, such as price increases. Inefficient practices can impact margins, including exchange rates, oil prices, union issues, government policies, on time delivery, quality control, inventory turnover, shrinkage, and warehousing. Your ability to recognize these potential issues and demonstrate your company's capability to provide solutions can be the catalyst you need to obtain the account.

Customers

> *"The purpose of a business is to find and keep a customer."*
> – Peter Drucker

Your purpose is to directly or indirectly assist your customer in achieving that objective. New business development is the lifeblood of any business, yet it must happen while maintaining the existing customer base.

In a previous chapter, we discussed the pareto principle (the 80/20 rule). The principle applies to a company's customer base as well, where 20% of their customers represent 80% of their revenue. Your ability to expand this percentage will position you as someone who provides values. This is your differentiator.

- Can you assist your customers to target the right customers?
- Which customers are the right ones? Why are they the right ones?
- What can you do to help your customers create loyalty?

- How can you expand their customer base?
- How can you help them position themselves positively in the customer's mind?
- What can you do to help your customer stand out from the competition?
- Can you provide more value towards this challenge than your competitor?

Competition

Competition is what drives innovation, but it can be a serious threat to the sustainability of any organization. Every executive is concerned with it. Your ability to provide insight into industry trends and the competitive landscape has intrinsic value that's not easy to obtain. The status quo and complacency are serious risks to all companies; your ability to provide insight into what is possible and how others in the industry are resolving these competitive pressures should not be undervalued.

- What are industry trends that your customer may not be aware of?
- What is the benefit of adopting these practices?
- How quickly can you help them implement these practices?
- What is their return on investment?
- What is the risk should they ignore these pressures?

Can you provide more value towards this challenge than your competitor can?

Globalization

According to the research by Steve Tappin and Andrew Cave in their book, " The Secrets of CEOs: 150 Global Chief Executives Lift the Lid on Business, Life and Leadership," globalization is one of the major concerns for today's CEOs.

Globalization is a progression of communication and integration between individuals, companies, and governments of diverse countries. It's a process driven by global commerce and investment, and it's supported by technology which expands beyond regional or national outlooks. The result is a unified and interdependent economy with unrestricted exchange of capital, goods, and services across countries.

This poses many potential problems for companies. They are confronted by global competitors, regulatory issues, labor relations, language barriers, cultural differences, accounting practices, operating procedures, and production. Clearly, this creates new opportunities and risks for the executive team.

Your ability to help an organization predict potential threats while guiding them through those threats makes you an indispensable ally.

- How do they find top talent abroad?
- How will they comply with government regulations across different countries?
- How do they measure a liveable wage across different countries?
- How do they ensure procedure compliance with various languages?
- How do they ensure respect is displayed within diverse cultures?
- How do they provide a uniform customer experience across the globe?
- Can you provide more value towards this challenge than your competitor can?

Regulatory

Regulatory can be defined as limitations imposed on the activities of a firm in compliance with the requirements of a regulatory agency. [25]

The result of a company's being non-compliant ranges from negative public perception to financial penalties to even jail time. This is a major concern to every CEO, and it poses a major risk to anyone who does not hold himself accountable to regulatory compliance. Consider Jeff Skilling, former CEO of Enron, presently serving 25 years for the failure to comply.

Each industry will have different regulatory controls to which they must adhere. These include GAAP or (general accepted accounting principles), workers compensation, labor laws, transportation of dangerous goods, occupational health and safety, food safety, and (as stated previously) Canada's Bill C-45.

Bill C-45 added Section 217.1 to the Criminal Code which reads:

"**217.1** Every one who undertakes, or has the authority, to direct how another person does work or performs a task is under a legal duty to take **reasonable steps** to prevent bodily harm to that person, or any other person, arising from that work or task." [Source : Canadian Centre for Occupational Health and Safety, http://www.ccohs.ca/oshanswers/legisl/billc45.html]

Most people won't want to let a judge interpret whether they had taken reasonable steps.

Providing insight and advice on how an executive can improve her safety and the safety of her employees while reducing the potential of high levies or even jail time is a valuable resource, and it certainly separates you from just selling products and taking orders.

- How can you help you customer stay compliant with regulatory issues?
- What can you do to improve worker safety?
- What can you do to reduce employee exposure to health and safety issues?
- Can you provide effective training to employees to reduce exposure?
- Can you provide more value towards this challenge than your competitor can?

Sustainability

Again, according to the research by Steve Tappin and Andrew Cave, decoding sustainability is another of the major concerns for today's CEOs.

The three pillars of sustainability are generally accepted as people, planet, and profit   (or economical, financial, or social), however, the tipping point has been reached on sustainability. Chief executives must now address the corporate environmentalism agenda, those who don't will be caught up in the coming years. Top CEOs are already looking beyond "green" to the commercial benefits of doing business responsibly in a wider sense. CEOs in the future will embrace sustainability and prioritize the raft of initiatives required to demonstrate that their companies are responsible and care about the societies in which they operate.

"Top leaders believe that doing "the right thing" is also great business in the long term and that all stakeholders will eventually call for businesses to embrace a role in society beyond respect for the environment. The good news is that the proliferation of best practice, and of fora in which to earn it, as well as the increasing level of concern among the wider population, mean that CEOs will be swimming with the tide in addressing the sustainability agenda.

Overall, the outlook for improved sustainability efforts from business looks quite promising at present, but the recent downturn in developed economies will undoubtedly be a sharp test of the commitment of every company." [26]

- Does your customer have a sustainability position?
- Can you assist them with this initiative?
- How is your product or service positioned for this directive?
- Can you help your customer position themselves as a leader in this forum?
- How can you assist them in differentiating their company from the competition?
- Can they achieve this initiative with minimal disruption to current systems?

- Can you provide more value towards this challenge than your competitor can?

If you follow the S.A.L.E.S. Formula™ in its proper sequence, at this point you will be ready to move to the fourth step in the formula: exposing the implications of the information you have gathered.

Through this process, you will have identified business drivers and pressures that your prospect may not have been aware of. If you've asked the right questions, your prospect will begin to see you as someone who can assist them in improving their internal and external pressures.

Before we move on to the fourth step, we need to discuss the art of listening. Most of us are great at hearing, but we could all improve our listening skills.

Listening

We are all guilty of one thing when it comes to listening: the majority of our thoughts are about ourselves. We continuously think about what we need or want, even when we are having an important conversation with key customers. Don't feel bad. We all are guilty of this at one point or another.

Research suggests that our minds think eight times faster than we can speak; however, we can listen at a rate of 400 to 500 words per minute and think at 1000 words per minute.

With these numbers in mind, it's easy to see how our prospect's mind could start to roam if we are speaking for any length of time; therefore it's very important that we continue to ask questions. When the customer is speaking, we can take their listening skills out of the equation.

Research suggests that salespeople do up to 60% of the talking. [27]

We listen at about 25% of our potential. We miss, ignore, forget, distort, or misunderstand 75% of what we hear. [28]

The foundation to the S.A.L.E.S. Formula™ is listening to what the prospect is saying when he is responding to your questions. Listening with your full attention is the primary skill you must have for sales success. Listen as if this were a million-dollar prospect who was just on the verge of giving you a major order. Listen as if there were no one else in the world to which you would rather listen at this moment than this prospect, and to what this prospect is saying. [29]

The Five Second Reply Rule

It's human nature to want to reply to a question or thought that has been presented to you immediately, both in an effort to show that you have the answer, as well as being preconditioned from childhood to respond when spoken to. In insightful selling, it's important to resist this urge and to implement the five second reply rule.

The five second reply rule says that you must wait five full seconds before responding to a question or expression of thought. This will demonstrate that you are listening to your prospect's questions or answers while taking a moment to process, consider, and contemplate before replying to him.

When you do respond, if you are not 100% certain what he is asking, repeat the question for clarification. This will ensure that you have not misunderstood, and give your prospect an opportunity to clarify.

You might respond with, "Mr. Customer, if I understand you correctly, you are concerned with the fluctuation in the market and this prevents you from making a decision. Is that correct?" Once the customer confirms that you clearly understand him, you position yourself as somebody who respects him. This builds trust and is the starting point to a long-term relationship.

Those with superior listening skills are more likely to build rapport, trust, and superior business relationships. It's been said that if you want someone to like you first, like them. Good listening demonstrates that you like and respect your prospect.

Guidelines to Effective Listening

- ✓ Determine each follow-up question upon the response of your prospect. You must be 100% focused on the prospect.
- ✓ Many people are afraid of confrontation, and therefore will not be as direct and open as someone whom you know on a personal basis. Listen to what is being said; however, what is not being said can be more important.
- ✓ Avoid the impulse to interrupt your prospect. Let him complete his thought and express himself fully before you respond.

- ✓ A short pencil is better than a long memory. Make sure that you write down what your prospect has said. This demonstrates professionalism and will assist you when summarizing the conversation to him.
- ✓ Remember your branding position and how you want to be thought of in the business world. Never compromise your integrity or professionalism.
- ✓ There is a difference between sympathy and empathy. Always demonstrate empathy towards the prospect's feeling, thoughts, and beliefs.
- ✓ Avoid stereotyping a prospect based on his appearance or intelligence level. Judge him based on what he says and how he behaves, not on how he looks or communicates. Listen without prejudice.

CHAPTER 9 – THE EXPOSE STEP
Expose the Problem

The S.A.L.E.S Formula™ is not about selling solutions to problems, because two changes have made this solution selling approach less useful:

1. The shift from the executive as a problem fixer to the executive as the opportunity creator.
2. The shift from selling value communication to selling value creation. [5]

Up to this point you have:

> **Step 1 –** <u>**Studied**</u> the industry and company before your first meeting.
> **Step 2 –** <u>**Asked**</u> the questions about their **organizational goals** and the **operations** of the company.
> **Step 3 –** <u>**Learned**</u> about their goals and operations to identify problems within their existing practices which they're not aware of.

The **4th step** in the S.A.L.E.S. Formula™ is "expose." These are questions that allow the prospect to recognize she has a problem and express the implication in detail. It gives her a chance to explain how this impacts her business. You do not want to tell her she has a problem, but through effective questions help her recognize she has one.

Exposing problems enables the prospect to recognize the implications that impact his objectives, as well as internal and external pressures. Your primary goal is to expose problems and their consequences to motivate the buyer to ask you for a solution.

Insightful selling, utilizing the S.A.L.E.S. Formula™, is centered on exposing the implication of the problem to the buyer. Most salespeople know how to ask general fact-finding questions, but most don't spend the time and effort necessary to learn of a problem and expose its implications. Once they have identified a problem, many start talking about the features of their products or going through a brochure's talking points.

This provides little value to the buyer. The objective of the fourth step is to expose opportunity and create value to the customer's business. In other words, your primary objective in this step is value creation.

Value Creation

The S.A.L.E.S. Formula™ is really about one thing: positioning you as an executive who creates value. Your primary objective is to assist the customer in achieving their goals and objectives by positioning the product or service you represent in a secondary role. Creating value is the differentiator to successful selling in the 21st century.

Following the S.A.L.E.S. Formula™ in its proper sequence should position you in the customer's mind as:

- One who understands his industry.
- One who is professional and asks relevant and thought-provoking questions.
- One who understands business and can assist them in being better.
- One who can help them meet their goals and objectives, thus providing value.

Creating value is the only way that the 21st century executive can differentiate himself in today's highly competitive, commodity-driven economy.

You need to continually ask yourself:

- Can you assist your customer in achieving their goals and objectives?
- Can you impact their income statement?
- Can you improve internal pressures?
- Can you improve external pressures?
- Can you help your customer enter new markets and drive new revenue?

There are two distinctive characteristics that position you as an insightful executive who creates value. The primary differentiator is you.

YOU

The sales professional-turned-executive is the differentiator. It is your ability to utilize the four executive skills to create value and impact your customer's business that sets you apart. As we discussed in an earlier chapter, the way you position yourself begins with the way you prospect, including your mannerisms and your style of dress. It all plays an important role in distinguishing you from the competition. The time you invest in understanding the 4 Cs – company, competition, customer, and contact person – will help you provide insight and create value.

Company

Your ability to study your customer's organization and understand their business goals and operations is the key driver to differentiating yourself and being able to provide and create value for them.

Competition

Knowledge of the competition and understanding their weaknesses lets you leverage and position your company as being strong where the competition is vulnerable.

Customer

Who is your customer's customer? What are they looking for? Your ability to help your customer meet their customer's needs is of value to them.

Contact

Your ability to talk in the language that your contact understands in relation to his or her personality type and your ability to build rapport quickly can expedite the selling process.

Your ability to address the four C's along with the four executive skills will position you as an expert in the eyes of the customer. Your expertise and professionalism will demonstrate value to your customer and position you as an executive with insight.

Your Company

Questions encourage the buyer to express his ideas, beliefs and feelings. When the customer states a problem to you, it is a fact; when you state a problem to him, it is your opinion.

Your goal is to guide the customer to identify key areas within their operational processes with a negative impact on their business. In 87.5% of the calls you make, buyers will not be aware that a problem exists. If they knew they had a problem, they would be in the 12.5% of buyers in the discontent stage; therefore, don't expect someone to realize he has a problem until you begin exposing the implication to him.

No need exists for the buyer until the buyer recognizes she has a need. Once the customer acknowledges that she has a problem and expresses a desire to change, many amateur salespeople begin to present a solution.

The insightful seller recognizes that this is where you begin to create value for the buyer. You would be doing both of you a disservice if you start solving her problems now.

Why? Because the real cost of the problem has not yet been identified. Your primary objective at this juncture is to raise the problem from "could change" to "must change."

By asking questions that expose the problem, while linking the implication to the bottom line, you are making the problem more important.. There is a greater financial implication associated with the problem, so the customer will feel it necessary to correct it.

Exposing problems is the most important step in the S.A.L.E.S. Formula™ because there is usually a financial implication to the problem. And remember, every buyer's responsibility is to directly or indirectly contribute to the company's bottom line.

Exposing the implication through questions creates three possibilities:

- ✓ It identifies an opportunity and its potential impact on the organization.
- ✓ It determines which internal and external pressures have the highest implication.
- ✓ It positions you as someone who can provide value.

The S.A.L.E.S. Formula™, when followed in its proper sequence, will move the client from a place of comfort to a place of discomfort. In a nutshell, you are helping the buyer identify a problem which is negatively impacting their business and then solving it with your product or service.

Exposing the implication with effective questions is difficult to prepare for, because the questions you ask are largely dependent upon the response the buyer gives.

These questions increase your chance of success, particularly with larger and more complex buyers, because they allow you to expose and expand the problem from a minor issue to a major issue. The buyer begins to see the problem as something that's worth solving and the buyer will recognize that investing time and energy into solving it will positively impact their bottom line.

Your proficiency with the four executive skills provides you with the insight to create, develop, and ask questions that **expose** inefficiencies within the internal and external pressures of the organization.

Objectives	R&D	Talent	Turnover	Sales & Marketing
Productivity	Culture	Customers	Competition	Health & Safety
Globalization	Regulatory	Sustainability	Systems	Technology

All of the categories above, which were discussed in the previous chapter, can be categorized into one of three primary categories in an organization:

Profits – These are problems that relate to the bottom line and have a negative effect on operating costs or the revenue-generating ability of the company.

Customers – These issues include anything to do with overall quality and satisfaction.

Employees – These are concerns regarding job satisfaction, turnover, and productivity.

What types of problems occur in these areas?

Profits – Decreased revenue, increased operational costs.

Customers – Decreased customer satisfaction, loss of customers.

Employees – Decreased employee satisfaction, loss of employees, decreased productivity. [30]

Each of these problems creates a negative implication for a company; your primary aim is to expose these issues by asking questions that produce dialogue where the buyer is recognizing the consequences.

It should be noted that, at times, you're going to return to asking about their internal and external pressures. This will uncover, establish, and develop the implication as necessary.

If you're in the sales training business, your primary target might be the VP of Sales. You would have developed questions which focus on internal pressures such as sales and marketing, organizational goals, and turnover, and external pressures like competitive forces. The following are some questions that you might use to expose the problem and its implication.

"Mr. Buyer, Can we go back to your (Pick the segment you have identified as having the greatest opportunity)? You expressed that margins are being eroded and your sales team is having a challenge with differentiation."

"What do you see as the long-term effect if this does not change?"

"What could you do to rectify this situation?" (This question will assist you in determining the space between what is presently happening within the organization and where they would like to be.)

"Have you addressed this issue in the past? How did you handle it?" (Your objective here is to determine what has happened in the past and why it was unsuccessful. What could have been done differently? How open are they to addressing this issue again?)

"What measures need to be implemented to solve this problem?" (This will determine the changes that the buyer is willing to address in order to ensure a successful resolution to the problem.)

"If this continues, how do you foresee this impacting your company's profitability?" (Finance is the language of business, and every decision either increases revenue or decreases profitability. This question will allow you to determine whether the buyer considers this to be an 'important to change' or 'urgent to change' issue.)

"Is this something that you consider important or urgent on your list of priorities?" (Many things are important when it comes to business; however, urgency is a different ball game. This question will provide you insight into the buyer's thought process.)

"How does this threaten your organizational objective of...?"
(This question encourages the buyer to consider the implication of not achieving the objective.)

The purpose is not only to gain information that exposes the implication of his problem or condition, but also to shape the buyer's thinking. You are attempting to open his mind to what is possible. To accomplish this, you need to have him consider the consequences, issues, and benefits in more depth than he has in the past.

Linking Questions

One of the best ways to build credibility and create change is to link the four executive skills with your questions to persuade the client's thinking. This accomplishes three things:

1. Obtaining additional information by the response that she provides.
2. Establishing you as an insightful executive and demonstrating your credibility.
3. Once the subconscious mind accepts something as true, change is more readily accepted.

Let's look at a few examples.

"Mrs. Customer, XYZ company (make sure it's not a direct competitor) found that when they reviewed their internal (pick one) process, they found approximately 9% of the tasks were incomplete and needed to be done from scratch. This cost them thousands of hours in labor. How has your company managed this process and have you measured the efficiencies in this area?"

By linking the success you had with XYZ Company, you build credibility while using social proof to influence the decision.

Social Proof

If the group of people who are performing a certain behavior is perceived to belong to the same or similar group, then one is more likely to conform to the group's behavior than if one does not identify with the group. (Cialdini, 2009) [31]

Another way to build credibility and create change is to link someone of influence – make sure your client would know and respect him – with your question to persuade the client's thinking.

"Mrs. Customer, Adon Rigg, creator of the S.A.L.E.S. Formula™, says that selling today is not about having a superior product or discovering problems and solving them, but about finding opportunities and creating value for the customer. Do you feel that your sales team has the knowledge and the skills necessary to succeed in the 21st century? Are they able to differentiate their offering to generate higher margins and avoid the commoditization of your product?"

When you associate a factual statement and link it with a question, your prospect hears the statement but concentrates on the questions. Unless the statement is unsubstantiated or completely out of left field, the factual statement is accepted as true and relevant, making your question relevant and important.

You primary objective is to have the customer recognize through your questions that they have a problem large enough to be resolved. To be successful, you need to expose the consequences of the problem in as many areas as possible. Insightful selling is about moving the customer from a position of satisfaction to a position of dissatisfaction and helping them identify practices, processes, and problems that, if rectified, will impact the financial viability of their organization.

Quoting people in a position of authority or using examples of similar customers (social proof) allows the buyer to feel secure in revealing that they, too, are experiencing similar challenges. Most people do not want to admit that they need to change; however, once they understand that others have done it, they are much more likely to accept the idea. This is usually something that happens subconsciously, but once they realize that they are not alone and others experience these challenges, they become more open to the idea of change.

Insightful selling is not about telling the buyer he has a problem, but creating an environment where the buyer realizes he has a problem and asks you for your suggestions on how to resolve the challenge.

You should only expose problems in areas that have implications you can solve. The best way to ensure you stay focused on their internal, external, and organizational objectives is to develop a **hypothesis** before your meeting (as discussed in previous chapter).

- Create a list of potential challenges and what the solutions to those problems might be.
- Determine what you need to learn before you begin to expose any potential problems.
- Decide what probable implications are affecting the buyer's bottom line.
- Link your "expose" questions to what the client is saying.

The following is another example of how to link phrases with questions:

Insightful Seller: You spoke earlier about the challenge of retaining your sales force. What impact is this having on sales?

Buyer: We are not maximizing the potential of each customer, because it takes time for the new representative to learn our business and develop a relationship with the customer.

Insightful Seller: How about training new hires. Does that impact resources?

Buyer: Yes. We need to invest time to train and get them up to speed.

Insightful Seller: According to Statistics Canada, it is estimated to cost 30% of an employee's salary to train a new hire. Considering this statistic, what do you estimate it is costing you financially each year with attrition?

Buyer: I have not really thought about that. I'm not sure.

Insightful Seller: Well, do you mind if we look at this for a moment?

Buyer: Sure.

Insightful Seller: What is the average annual salary of one of your sales representatives?

Buyer: It ranges from rep to rep, but I would estimate $50,000 each.

Insightful Seller: How many reps are you losing each year?

Buyer: It varies every year, but I would estimate two or three.

Insightful Seller: Would it be fair then to say that the attrition rate of your sales force turnover is costing you over $45,000 per year, not to mention the hidden financial impact of lost revenue opportunities?

Buyer: That sounds fair.

Insightful Seller: Assuming you work on an average profit margin of 30%, that means you need $150,000 in sales to make up for the $45,000 in lost profit.

Buyer: I've tried everything to keep them, but I keep losing them to the competition.

Insightful selling in the 21st century is about peeling the onion to expose the core implication of the buyer's current operational processes. In the above example, we did not discuss a solution, only the implication or consequence of losing the sales force. Can you see how, in the example above, the insightful seller could take the conversation down many different paths? I must reiterate: we do **not want to offer a solution** at this juncture. We want to continue to expose all the implications that this issue brings to the buyer.

- ✓ Expose questions need to center around the internal and external pressures of their business. That is the purpose of your call.
- ✓ Expose questions need to guide the customer to the conclusion that you intend.
- ✓ Expose questions must uncover and expose the negative aspects of their current situation.
- ✓ Expose questions must be relevant and thought-provoking.
- ✓ Expose questions capture the language that creates the desire to take action.
- ✓ Expose questions need to create an atmosphere that inspires ideas, solutions, and possibilities.
- ✓ Expose questions must be relevant to the buyer and their company.
- ✓ Expose questions cannot be evasive or disrespectful.
- ✓ Expose questions must move you towards a desired outcome.
- ✓ Expose questions need to make the customer think of the problem or solution that you want them to think about.

- ✓ Expose questions have the ability to influence and direct the buyer's thinking.

- ✓ Expose questions position you as an expert in the mind of the customer.
- ✓ Expose questions utilize the language that motivates the action and thought process the salesperson intends to create.
- ✓ Expose questions build rapport and allow you to ask clearer and more precise questions.
- ✓ Expose questions direct your customer's thought process through the words you use.
- ✓ Expose questions are designed to peel away to the core of the problem.
- ✓ Expose questions cause the customer to think of their business in a deeper and more profound perspective.

In order to expose the implication to the fullest, you must be comfortable with the four executive skills we discussed throughout this book.
Let review them once more.

Executive Insight
Understand the language of business and how to make decisions that improve the financial viability of an organization.

Industry Knowledge
Having spent the time necessary to understand the buyer's business, be able to identify the most likely pressures within their business that your product or service can rectify.

Product Knowledge
Knowledge of your product goes deeper than its features. What financial benefit can you bring to the buyer's bottom line?

Questioning Skills
Ask impactful questions which pertain to the internal and external drivers of an organization. The objective is to create opportunities by providing value for the customer that positively impacts the company's income statement.

Questions that expose the implications cause the buyer to think about their business in multiple layers. This can position the executive as one who has insight and can provide value by affecting the organization's ability to generate revenue or reduce expenditures.

In the majority of situations from the customer's perspective, there's little that differentiates your product or service from the competition. Your ability to utilize the four executive skills is the differentiator and positions you as someone who creates value.

If you sell product to a problem, it goes to price. You need to identify opportunities to impact your customer's business as discussed throughout this book.

The S.A.L.E.S. Formula™ concentrates on two main objectives:

✓ Find, create, and grow dissatisfaction until the pain associated with changing surpasses the pleasure of continuing with the status quo.
✓ Utilize your executive skills to obtain the information required to assist them in achieving their corporate, regional, or individual goals and objectives.

Determine Your Value, the $1,000,000 Question

How much would the customer pay for the meeting you just had? The more they would have paid equals the value you provided. That is the $1,000,000 question and your measuring stick to determine the success of your call.

CHAPTER 10 – THE SOLVE STEP
Presenting the Solution

"The 21st Century buyer will choose to purchase from you because of the expertise and value you provide over the competition."
– Adon Rigg

Up to this point you have:

> **Step 1 – <u>Studied</u>** the industry and company before your first meeting.
> **Step 2 – <u>Asked</u>** the questions about their **organizational goals** and the **operations** of the company.
> **Step 3 – <u>Learned</u>** about their goals and operations to identify problems within their existing practices which they're not aware of.

Step 4 – <u>Exposed</u> their issues using questions that allow the prospect to recognize they have a problem and express the implication in detail.

The 5th and final step in the S.A.L.E.S Formula™ is to **solve** the customer's issues.

If you have followed the S.A.L.E.S. Formula™ in its proper sequence, you will have brought the buyer from a state of comfort to a state of discomfort. Effective solution questions will allow the buyer to discover for herself the benefit that a solution will provide her.

People are more inclined to value and invest in something they ask for rather than something you freely offer them. Solution questions are designed to motivate the buyer to state a clear need for a resolution. These questions focus the buyer's attention on the value that your solution will provide.

It's important to understand that the primary difference between a solution question and all other sales questions is that solution questions are based on value, and not discovery, investigation, or exploration.

The solution sequence of the S.A.L.E.S. Formula™ should be enjoyable and inspiring because it is focused on possibilities and opportunities.

1. Solution questions allow the buyer to link value to the solution.

2. Solution questions allow the buyer to widen his perception of value.

3. Solution questions inspire the buyer to find the value a solution to his problem provides.

4. Solution questions allow the buyer to express the benefits of a solution to his problem.

5. Solution questions allow the buyer to feel like part of the solution, and that makes him more committed to the successful outcome.

Asking solution questions determine if the buyer believes there is value in a possible solution. Timing is extremely important at this juncture, because if the buyer has not recognized a problem, then a solution question will not provide the impact it's intended to provide. In asking solution-based questions, the buyer should discover for himself the benefit that a solution will provide for him.

You're creating anticipation and excitement in the mind of the buyer with your solution questions. An example of solution questions might be:

"From a financial perspective, how would rectifying this issue benefit your division?"

"What is the benefit in solving this issue?"

"How important is it to solve this issue?"

"What kind of savings do you foresee annually if this is solved?"

"How else would this benefit you?"

"How much more productivity would this mean to your department?"

"If we reduce expenditures by 10%, what would that mean annually?"

"By eliminating this process, how much time will you save per day, week, month, year?"

You should not need to ask more than a few solution questions before the buyer has recognized that you have a solution to the discomfort that's been identified. When the buyer is responding to your solution questions, she is inadvertently selling herself on the benefits of the solution.

The definition of a benefit is a product or service that improves someone's life or business. Who doesn't want to improve, remove, or eliminate their current situation when faced with a problem?

Recent Huthwaite's research shows that in 63% of sales calls, solutions are offered before the customer states that they have a need. [32]

Benefits

"Buyers buy benefits."
– Adon Rigg

Benefits make the buyer's life easier. They reduce pain or increase pleasure, either directly or indirectly. For example, purchasing an extended warranty provides the buyer the security of not making a poor purchasing decision, thus reducing potential pain.

When purchasing a new vehicle, someone may purchase the external keypad on the driver side door to unlock his car. The main benefit may be different for each individual buyer. One may make the extended purchase decision because of the convenience should he lock his keys in the car. Another buyer may find this a secondary benefit; however, the primary benefit to her might be not having to carry her keys around with her all the time.

Positioning Benefits

A benefit is only a benefit if the buyer considers it to be one. The insightful seller understands that benefits are subjective. So it's imperative to present benefits from the customer's point of view. You want the buyer to easily identify that your solution will benefit, help, or improve his situation.

Benefits are 100% of the reason that a buyer will make a purchasing decision; however, many salespeople focus on features (how the product works, how it is better than another product, how it is cheaper). This will not motivate the buyer to make a purchasing decision. The buyer wants to know how her life will be improved, and in a B2B (business to business) scenario, that improvement needs to impact her income statement.

The Importance of Benefits

✓ It is important to remember that buyers buy the benefit, not the feature.

✓ Benefits focus on customer needs. Features focus on the product.

The following is an example of how you can position your product's features in a way that demonstrates to the customer their benefit.

Remember, we are always trying to show how we can positively impact their company's bottom line; this can be done continually throughout the meeting by directly and indirectly linking your product or service to one or more of the five sections on the income statement.

Features	Benefit
ten-year warranty	reduce capital expenditures
50 km to the gallon	extended gas consumption by 20%
easy to navigate website	increase customer viewership, increase online purchases
hands-free navigation	reduces accident and fatalities

✓ Just because one customer perceives it to be a benefit does not mean all customers will perceive it to be a benefit.

The main benefit that the buyer is purchasing in the 21st century is you. The expertise and insight you provide over the competition is the main reason the buyer is going to make a purchasing decision. The competition, in most cases, is trying to find a buyer in the discontent stage (which is less than 12.5 % of buyers). This is a formula for selling on price, making the salesperson irrelevant and his product a commodity in the eyes of the buyer.

The S.A.L.E.S. Formula™, if followed in its proper sequence, will distinguish you as an expert who adds value to their organization. Your discipline and commitment to excellence are evident to the buyer with the knowledge you display through the research and studying you have done. You'll have asked specific questions about the goals and operational procedures of their company which has allowed you to understand how to position your offering to improve the internal or external pressures that impact their income statement. With effective questioning skills, you have exposed problems and implications the buyer didn't see before. The final step is to provide a solution to the buyer.

Summarize Before Presenting Solutions

Before you offer solutions, you should summarize your conversation with them, to ensure you have understood the buyers' requests, concerns and expectations for the future. The following is an example of how to ensure that you and the buyer are on the same page.

"Mrs. Buyer, I would like to summarize our conversation to ensure that I have understood you correctly and make certain that we are on the same page. Does that sound fair? Great, you have XYZ objectives this year and believe that retaining your sales force and improving their skill set will be key contributors to meeting your objectives. You believe that educating them on the S.A.L.E.S. Formula™ is a step in that direction; however, you would like to see special emphasis on utilizing new technology for prospecting and improve questioning skills. Is that correct?"

The next step is for you to determine whether this will be a large sale or a smaller sale, in term of dollar figures. You will also need to determine if the buyer has the direct authority to finalize the deal, or if other key decision makers need to be included. This will determine your next move.

Presenting a Solution

Presentation skills are an art and require practice. This is why so few salespeople are great at them.

Position Yourself

You should be positioning yourself every day of your professional career; presenting is no different. The people you meet will make a judgement call about your ability and character within the first five seconds of meeting you. They will then give you another 25 seconds to change their opinion. Nothing is neutral! Everything counts. "Never let them see you sweat," to borrow from an old deodorant commercial.

Preparation is essential; developing a powerful presentation is a process that takes time and strategy. A 20-minute presentation requires a minimum of 30 minutes preparation per slide. A 10-slide presentation will require at least five hours of design, thought, and planning.

Practice, and then practice some more. Your delivery is imperative to your success; the slides should create curiosity and optimism in the minds of those viewing. Do not read your slides off the projection screen. If you need to view the slides, place your laptop in a position where you can see the presentation without looking at the screen. You are on stage and need to fully engage the audience. Avoid anything that distracts your body positioning and eye contact from being focused on those in attendance.

Have fun and allow your delivery to reflect your personality. Interact with the audience like you would with a group of colleagues having a lunch meeting, not too formal and not too casual. Just be professional.

Stories and Assumptions

People think in pictures, not words. Words are simply a tool we use to communicate with one another. Another word for pictures is metaphor. When communicating with someone, using an example or story is a powerful way to express your point of view. A story cannot be argued. This is a powerful form of influence that communicators use when they want to bypass resistance.

> *"People do business with us, choose to be with us, or select us as the supplier more on the basis of the state we induce in them than any of the content we might offer."* [33]
> – Sue Knight

Using a story, quote, or metaphor can be very influential, as it bypasses conscious opposition and grips our subconscious minds, which are compliant to instructions.

For example, you could describe a conversation you had with a buyer to potential customers. Tell a story about how the buyer was initially reluctant to make a purchasing decision, but she then decided that few people create change by staying with the status quo. Ultimately you have used this story as a way to tell the customer what they should do without taking any responsibility. The customer will accept the quote subconsciously as true without challenging your right to provide it.

Assumptions

You might be thinking how you can use metaphors more effectively in your everyday life.

What I have just done is inadvertently asked you to think about metaphors in your everyday life. Once you read and accept the suggestion, you are then subconsciously accepting all the other assumptions associated with the original statement.

As an example, the original statement assumes:

- ✓ That you can use metaphors more effectively.
- ✓ That you can use metaphors every day.
- ✓ That you want to use them in your everyday life.
- ✓ That you can think about metaphors.
- ✓ That you want to think about metaphors.

Assumptions are highly influential and can be a dominant force in achieving your objectives. They are very effective in presentations when you want the attendees to be accountable. The response would be dramatically different if you ask the question, "Can you make a commitment to this?" vs "What commitment can you make to this?"

Engagement

Making a connection with the audience to keep them interested and engaged is your top priority. Your presentation should be divided into three sections: opening, content, and closing.

A. The opening should address three questions to gain their attention.

Why are you here? Who are you? Your opening comments should not be something you take lightly, but it is carefully considered and rehearsed. This will set the direction and the tone for the remainder of the meeting. Example: "Hello, everyone. My name is Adon Rigg, and I am with Insightful Selling Solutions. We specialize in (Value Proposition) assisting sales professionals to create value for their customers and increase profitability."

Remember that communication is 55% nonverbal, 38% tone of voice, and 7% words. How you look and the way you say it constitutes for 93% of your first impression.

WIIFT – What's in it for them? Remember this is not about you and putting more money into your jeans. It is about them and improving their internal or external drivers. People dislike change and will not be open to it unless they believe it will benefit them and make their lives better. Example: "XYZ Company was able to gain access to the C-suite of their prospects and reduce the selling time by 77% in just 12 months."

What we'll discuss today. This is where you set the agenda and the expectations for the meeting. Make the agenda benefit-oriented (WIIFT) and address where you're going and how you plan to get there. Setting the agenda is very important because you are there above all else to entertain and engage.

The reward is an audience that gets inspired and motivated to embrace the change you're selling. Failure to set the agenda will result in disengaged participants because they don't know what to expect.

Ask a question immediately. Before you dive into your presentation, ask a question to get the audience involved and interested in the process. This is an effective way to engage your audience and give them an opportunity to participate. You can connect their thoughts to specific points later in your presentation. People are more inclined to believe something they say than something they are told.

Questions to ask?

The question you ask should be the beginning of your presentation, guiding the audience's thoughts toward the topic you are addressing. Ultimately it positions the relevance of your speech and makes your audience immediately engaged and focused.

- What do you think is the biggest challenge to profitable growth?
- How many of you would like to increase margin?
- How many of you are having a challenge differentiating your offering from that of the competition?

B.   The Content of your presentation

It's important that you present your material in a logical and systematic way, to lead your audience from one thought through to the next. The simplest way to accomplish this is with a heading in your presentation followed by one bullet point at a time. Do not display the next bullet point until you have completed everything you want to discuss with the present bullet point. Your audience will read ahead and begin wondering or presuming what you're going to say, so don't take their attention away from the present point you're trying to make.

When transitioning from one point to another, ensure that you take your audience along with you by clearly emphasizing the conclusion of one thought and the beginning of another. Make a statement supported with a slide on your presentation. An example might be something like:

- ✓ "Now we know that technology is changing at an incredible rate, but the question is how we can prepare for the future. Let's look at this."

- ✓ "If this is the state of the current situation, how should we adjust our plans?"

C.   The Closing of Your Presentation

Closing is a major component to a presentation and should be carefully considered and practiced. Summarize your key points, connect them to the theme of your speech, and close with a strong statement which invokes passion and a call to action.

Consider all Personality Types

If you are presenting to an individual, you should develop your presentation towards the individual's personality type. When designing a presentation for a group, it is good to incorporate content that reaches each individual personality type. In group scenarios, you should still consider the personality of the main decision maker and cater the presentation in their direction.

What works for one prospect will not necessarily work for another. Most salespeople present in the style that they would like to be presented to without considering the different conversational styles of each prospect. As we discussed in an earlier chapter, there are four personality types, and each one receives and interacts with the world in different ways. Be sure to consider this when preparing and delivering a presentation.

> **Relater.** When presenting to relaters, be sensitive to the people side of the business. Include them in the discussion and ask for their opinions and feelings about the material. Demonstrate that your solution will be inclusive to all departments. Be sure to include

references and testimonials from other satisfied customers. These individuals like regular routine and enjoy the status quo. The relater personality responds slowly, is generally quieter, slightly indecisive, and concerned about being liked.

Socializer. When presenting to socializers, it is important to consider that recognition of their achievements is a motivator to them. They are extroverts with strong relationship skills and expressive personalities. They are achievement-oriented and like plaques, trophies, awards, authority, and control. When presenting your solutions, demonstrate how they will achieve greater success and recognition. Create an environment that is entertaining and fun, while selling the sizzle.

Analyzer. When presenting to thinker/analyzers, consider that they tend to be logical, crave information, and are detail-oriented. Analyzers are thinkers and demand accurate and reliable information. Support material and documentation containing technical data is important to them. Analyzers take their time to consider, ponder, and work out any issues. These individuals are task-oriented and introverted in their demeanor. Provide them with details, details, and more details; they like to make the correct decision and are proud of doing the job right. Do not rush them for decisions, but establish a follow-up time and respond quickly to their requests for more information.

Director. When presenting to directors, you must be quick and to the point. Don't waste their valuable time on small talk. Provide them with the facts, and demonstrate measurable results with options. The director is concerned with the bottom line, achieving more and getting the job done on time and on budget. They are extremely impatient and candid and dislike the details. Demonstrate how the job will be done faster and better. Expect a decision quickly. The director personality likes to dominate every situation, therefore expect your presentation to be interrupted with questions or comments.

Preventing Objections

- ✓ Objection handling is a much less important skill than most training makes it out to be.
- ✓ Objections, contrary to common belief, are more often created by the seller then the customer.

✓ In the average sales team, there is usually one sales person who receives ten times as many objections per selling hour than another person in the same team.

✓ Skilled people receive fewer objections because they have learned objection prevention, not objection handling. [34]

The more objections you receive during your presentation, the less likely you are to make a sale. Therefore it is important to consider all potential objections and address them in your presentation. By staying completely focused on the benefits and value that you are bringing to the table, objections should be minimal, if at all.

Objections are most likely to occur when additional people have been brought to the presentation who don't understand the internal or external pressures enough to identify the costs associated with them. Before you present a solution, ensure that everyone in the room fully understands the situation. This should be addressed at the beginning of your presentation by reviewing the business case for change.

It is important that each individual in the room begins to recognize you as an expert and trusted advisor, an insightful executive who can provide value to his business and help him achieve his goals and objectives. Buyers make a purchasing decision because what transpires in their company matters. They desire professionals who are confident, reliable, ethical, and professional who can direct them through every step during the process.

When your presentation is in line with improving their bottom line, you become relevant and integral to the successful execution of strategic objectives.

When your presentation is focused on creating value, you position yourself as an expert who offers a distinct advantage over the competition, and pricing is not the determining factor.

Buyers are not concerned about the price you charge when you provide value that impacts their responsibility, and in the 21st century that is achieved by:

✓ Demonstrating how they can achieve their goals and objectives.

✓ Providing them with a sustainable competitive advantage.

✓ Improving internal and external pressures.

✓ Helping them do more with less.

10-20-30 Rule

Venture capitalist Guy Kawasaki introduced a general rule for effective presentations. He referred to it as the 10-20-30 rule.

Although not everyone may use it, it does provide a guideline for presenters. It begins with the rule of ten. Using ten slides during the presentation is recommended by Mr. Kawasaki. This may not sound like enough to you, but remember that you are not trying to "close a deal" but to present an idea or concept. More than ten slides could result in confusion and make the presentation too complex for most people. Nobody can be inspired or motivated if they are confused.

You may be wondering how you can get the information you want onto ten slides, and the answer is that you can't. A presentation is a presentation, a book is a book, and a document is a document. They all vary in degrees of information; you'll have an opportunity to provide all your information, I promise.

The rule of twenty is the recommended time that you have to make your presentation. After 20 minutes your audience will begin to lose interest and may start looking at their smartphones. Remember – again – you are not there to close the deal but to inspire and motivate. In any event, if you fail to inspire, it is very unlikely that you will be able to close the deal. Although the meeting may be scheduled for an hour, you have to allow for inevitable interruptions, latecomers, and those who need to leave early. Therefore, leaving room for these possibilities, as well as allowing for questions and answers, is a wise decision. If this extends into social discussion, you will know that the people are engaged and inspired.

The rule of thirty means using a minimum size thirty font. **It is a good idea that your audience can see what is written!**

Have you ever been to a presentation where the presenter says, "I know you can't see this, but…" This is the fastest way to lose both the attention and credibility of your audience. Your presentation slides are a tool to reinforce your point, not for you to have to repeat it. Use them to stimulate and engage your audience. Viewers should be able to see the font from any seat in the room. Also, keep lights on so that the focus is on you and your presentation, not just on the screen. As well, a darkened room can create a sluggish and even drowsy atmosphere, which is not what you want.

When presenting data is part of your presentation, you must be clear and transparent, so that you do not appear to be deliberately skimming over the issue. Data slides should focus on the significance (benefit) of the data rather than information on the data itself. If extended focus on data is necessary, it would be best to distribute a detailed printout to each attendee for a detailed discussion. Remember, the "analyzer" personality will love the process involving data, but other personalities will not. Data can easily turn a presentation into a debate, so be careful to use data only if it truly benefits and enhances your main points. Explain your vision and remember the "less is more" rule. Using a percentage number along with pictures can often help get the point across without too much data. If, for example, you were trying to demonstrate that 50% of the population is female, consider showing a female with 50% written beside her. This is much more effective than a bar graph.

General Proposal

The final step in presenting your solution is the preparation and delivery of your proposal. It is important to distribute the proposal after completing your oral presentation and any question-and-answer period. This will prevent the audience from distracting themselves by viewing your presentation while you are speaking.

The general proposal consists of a maximum 10 pages and is an essential part of the S.A.L.E.S. Formula™ and is an extended version of your presentation with more detail. It should be short, concise, and well-written, containing no more than five to ten (not including cover page and appendix) pages, double-spaced, with a 12 point font.

The following is an outline that provides a systematic process that supports a positive outcome.

1. Cover page
2. Executive Summary   (one page maximum)
3. Situation Analysis   (one page maximum
4. Goals and Objectives   (one page maximum)
5. Challenge and Implications (two pages maximum)
6. Recommended Solutions   (three pages maximum)
7. Appendix

Cover Page: The cover page should consist of your:

- ✓ Prospect's name. (Mrs. Buyer)
- ✓ Customer's Company name. (XYZ Company)
- ✓ Value proposition. (Differentiate the Sales Force and Eliminate the Price-Driven Sale)
- ✓ Your company. (Insightful Selling Solutions)

Executive Summary

This is a maximum one-page summary with an overview of your proposed solution, along with the benefits of formulating a business relationship with your company. This is the most read section of your general proposal and should be well-written, concise, and benefit-focused, detailing the buyer's desired objective and the benefits of working with your organization.

Situation Summary

This section should only address the current situation of the company, including internal and external pressures. Keep it one page in length, containing industry and company analysis pertinent to the information obtained from your initial meeting. It must summarize the buyers, target market, products, competitive advantage, and industry trends.

Goals and Objectives

This is the future-oriented section of the proposal and should specify organizational and divisional objectives that are on the urgent list of your buyer's priorities. Follow it with goals that are important, but not necessarily urgent; you will want to highlight the points that will make the greatest impact on their business.

- ✓ Increase profit by 3%
- ✓ Expand top line growth by 12%
- ✓ Improve R&D innovation
- ✓ Obtain LEED gold certification
- ✓ Reduce freight expenditures by 5%
- ✓ Outsource raw materials division

This is the section that buyers are concerned with. These issues reflect the greatest responsibilities to their portfolio and impact both top line and bottom line organizational and divisional objectives.

Challenge and Implications

This is an important section, as it exposes the problems and implications that you identified during the interview process. You should align organizational and divisional objectives with the impact they have on the bottom line. Documenting the implications clearly in bullet form provides the greatest visual impression.

- ✓ Stagnant top line growth over the last 24 months.
- ✓ Operational expenditures exceed x% of net sales.
- ✓ Turnover has increased 22% over the last 12 months.
- ✓ Customer satisfaction is down by 12%.
- ✓ Fill rates are less than 88%.
- ✓ Sales force unable to differentiate themselves from the competition.

The greater the list you provide, the better. Your objective at this point is **not** to provide solutions, but to expose and expand each implication to its fullest extent. The goal is to have the buyer recognize that problems definitely need to be addressed, and that the consequences have a real financial implication on the bottom line.

Recommended Solutions

This section must include all relevant information about your product or service and the benefit it provides. The benefit must address the problems and implications that you addressed during the interview process and further expand upon your oral presentation (if you provided one). Include a complete financial analysis of the problem and proposed solution, implementation plan, contributing members, including anticipated timelines and locations, if appropriate to this buyer.

The higher the perceived risk, the less likely you are to obtain their business. Therefore the conclusion of your presentation must include case studies, references, and a client list. Include any information that eliminates the potential objection of risk, finances, time, resources, and your ability to support the business.

Appendix

This section is to provide additional information that is relevant but not necessarily important to the proposal. Think brochures, catalogs, and industry reports.

Simplify the Decision

Building trust is the easiest way to gain commitment and move the process forward. By presenting to all the key players, you have assembled a case for change, identified problems, and created opportunity for their organization. You now need to ask yourself what possible objections could stall or derail the deal.

Build a Bridge

It does not necessarily need to be a yes or no decision. Have you ever been walking down the street and had a homeless person ask you for a twenty? For most of us, the answer would be no. However, most of us have been asked for change and given it. Why? The risk potential is minimal.

For the buyer, it's sometimes about the risk. Propose a trial at a certain location for an extended period of time to evaluate and measure if this solution is, in fact, what they hope it to be. It is a step in the right direction.

Payment Options

Sometimes it's about the money. Consider offering unique and inventive payment options like "30 day, no payment," "interest free for 90 days," or extended terms or rebates.

Whatever you do, don't compromise the positioning of your brand by offering your service at a lower price. Price objections are simply a lower perceived value, and this can be offset by providing additional value, such as time, resources, and consulting.

Closing

You don't close a customer, but open a relationship. If all goes according to plan, you will open a long-term one. The S.A.L.E.S. Formula™ is designed to position you as an expert and create a mutually beneficial relationship.

Closing is an old-school term that is more about defeating and beating a customer through tricks, manipulation, and sheer willpower. The old adage "always be closing" so perfectly depicted in the movie, "Glengarry Glen Ross," is no longer acceptable, and research suggests that the concept of closing does not play a critical role in a larger sale.

Confirming

Confirming is simply receiving permission to move the sales process forward. It is part of the formula and should be the obvious next step to both the seller and the buyer. You are simply asking the buyer if she would agree that the next step should be a purchasing decision.

If you have followed the S.A.L.E.S. Formula™ in its proper sequence, the buyer will have stated the benefit of finding a solution and be completely open to your suggested solution. All you have to do is ask for the order. The biggest obstacle to asking for the order is **you**.

Research suggests that over 70% of salespeople fail to ask for the order. By simply asking for the order in a non-manipulative and honest way, you will increase your success ratio exponentially. There are many ways to ask the same question; find one that is comfortable for you. Where do we go from here? What do you see as the next step? Are you open to testing/trying/starting this in a test location for 30 days? You can ask in a multitude of ways, but the important thing is to ask.

If the customer says no, then it's possible that he simply needs additional information. If you have followed the S.A.L.E.S. Formula™ correctly, then a return on investment has been presented and opening the relationship is simply a formality. It's common sense to spend a dollar to make two.

Confirming is not an event but part of the formula that started at the study stage. You should accept nothing less than a 70% success rate. What is your ratio? What part of the S.A.L.E.S. Formula™ gives you the greatest challenge? Practice makes perfect.

The 21st Century Insightful Executive

Selling in the 21st century is about thinking differently. It's about becoming an insightful executive through value creation for the buyer.

It's about impacting their income statement. It starts by recognizing the seven game changers that have transformed the world of selling.

1. Internet
2. Best practices
3. Commoditization
4. Inflation
5. Changing demographics
6. Sales 2.0
7. Web 3.0

The foundation to the S.A.L.E.S. Formula™ is your commitment to the four executive skills. These provide you with the tools necessary to create value for the buyer and will distinguish you as an expert and trusted advisor.

Product Knowledge

A product that is part of your portfolio may not be innovative from your standpoint. But you must look at the product from the perspective of the buyer. What benefit does it provide? What problem does it solve? What are the potential savings that your product can provide your buyer?

Think in terms of internal pressures such as occupational health and safety, compliance, productivity, culture, processes, turnover, talent, R&D, and sales and marketing. Look at external pressures such as customer demands, regulatory, sustainability, competition, globalization, supply chain, technology, and suppliers.

Industry Knowledge

You have an advantage over your buyer, because you have studied their industry and have the privilege of working with various companies within that sector. This provides you with insight into what excellence looks like. You can gauge where the buyer's company measures up in comparison. If one company has a problem in a particular area, the likelihood that other companies experience those same pressures is high. If a solution works for one buyer, it will probably work for other.

The knowledge you have about their industry and how your offering is presently positioned in their industry is the starting point to determine they have a need for your product. The question remains, "Why should I change the status quo and deal with you and your company?" The answer is your ability to understand the income statement while using your product knowledge to make an impact on their bottom line.

Executive Insight

To position yourself as an executive, you will need to learn the language of business. The language of any and all businesses is financial in nature. Whether you are calling on the CEO or the purchaser of office supplies, your prospect has an obligation to make a positive impact to her company's income statement. Your responsibility is to assist your prospect in meeting his or her mandate and to understand where you can make the most substantial impact to their business. In order to clearly determine how your product or service can positively impact the prospect's profit and loss statement, it is important to have a fundamental understanding of this very important financial measure.

Questioning Skills

Your ability to utilize your product knowledge, industry knowledge, and executive insight to ask effective and impactful questions is the key to successful selling in the 21st century. Questioning skills help you learn their processes and identify how to positively impact your prospect's income statement. Spend the necessary time to gain a working knowledge of their industry and to identify how your product can be positioned to achieve one or both of the following objectives.

a) Improve a current problem they're experiencing or uncover the problem they didn't know they had.
b) Discover what their goals and objectives are for the company and their specific department for that year.

Your questioning skills are essential to discovering the operational inefficiencies within a company and the goals or objectives that company is striving to meet for that specific year.

Selling the S.A.L.E.S. Formula™ is the differentiator for successful selling in the 21ˢᵗ century.

Study – Do your research before you make your sales call, because it is all about pre-call planning, positioning, and prospecting. These skills contribute to over 70% of your success, even before you've had your first meeting.

Ask – The GO ASK process will ensure that you're asking questions created around a hypothesis to provoke, inspire, and motivate the buyer to desire change.

Learn – How you can impact the buyer's bottom line always aligns with their organizational goals and operational processes.

Expose – Reveal the implications or consequences of their current condition through your questioning process. Challenge the status quo.

Solve – Once the buyer recognizes a problem, present your solution using your product or service. The S.A.L.E.S. Formula™ doesn't close customers; it opens relationships.

Building a bridge from no relationship to creating a customer can take a day, week, month or a year. Always think about the bottom-line of your business and the buyer's business. Follow the S.A.L.E.S. Formula™ and recognize that each step is dependent on the effective execution of the other. The differentiator in the 21st century is **you.** Selling, like any other skill, requires practice and continuous improvement. You only have to be average to earn an average income.

Consider obtaining a professional designation from Sales and Marketing Executive International (www.smei.org). Receive your CSE (Certified Sales Executive) designation or consider the CSP (Certified Sales Professional) designation. Either demonstrates a commitment to the profession, and by my estimation, they will one day be a prerequisite to obtaining employment.

Success is up to you

"Opportunity is missed by most people because it is dressed in overalls and looks like work."
– *Thomas Edison*

"Success is your dreams with work clothes on."
– *Unknown*

The S.A.L.E.S. Formula™ is a tool that simplifies the selling process. Becoming an insightful executive will differentiate you in the mind of the buyer as you are no longer selling product, but selling your expertise and insight to maximize their revenue and decrease expenses. Failure to differentiate yourself as an insightful executive is to delegate yourself as an order-taker. Buyers need professionals who understand their business. They want professionals who can help them achieve their goals and objectives. They want assistance eliminating internal or external pressures. Just selling product will not meet their expectations; that approach will always lead the conversation to price.

Differentiate yourself and utilize the S.A.L.E.S Formula™. Be an asset to the buyer's organization and to your own. If you're not an asset, then you must be an expense, and every business looks to eliminate an expense.

Good Luck and Good Selling!

Planning and Preparation

<u>Industry</u>

    A. What are the estimated annual sales for this industry?

_____

_____

    B. What are the estimated annual sales for this industry within your designated territory or region?

_____

_____

    C. What are the common internal pressures experienced with in this industry?

        1.

        2.

        3.

        4.

        5.

    D. What are the common external pressures experienced within this industry?

        1.

        2.

3.

4.

5.

Company

A. What are the estimated annual sales for this Company?

_____

_____

B. Is this prospect a global, multinational, national, provincial, state, or regional company?

_____

_____

C. How is this prospect positioned in the industry?

_____

_____

D. What differentiates this company from its competitors?

_____

_____

E. What is your hypothesis for this account? (Assumptions of their issues, problems, and opportunities)

_____

_____

F. What are the estimated potential sales for this account per year?

_____

_____

G. How many locations do they have?

_____

_____

H. How long have they been in business?

_____

_____

I. Who is their current supplier?

_____

_____

J. What are their current supplier's strengths?

_____

_____

K. What are their current supplier's weaknesses?

_____

_____

<u>Contact</u>

A. What is your contact's job title?

_____

_____

B. What do you know about this individual?

_____

_____

C. How long have they been with the company?

_____

_____

D. How many years experience in the industry do they have?

_____

_____

E. What are their hobbies?

_____

_____

F. Are they most likely an analyzer, expresser, director, or relater personality type?

_____

_____

G. Have you performed an advanced Google search? Yes or No

H. Have you performed a Linkedin advanced search? Yes or No

I. Have you looked for them on Facebook?   Yes or No

J. Have you looked to see if they are on Twitter?   Yes or No

Initial phone call planner

A. Based on your personality assumption, what three traits must you demonstrate during the initial contact?

_____

_____

B. What is your opening statement?

_____

_____

_____

_____

_____

C. What is your Value Proposition Statement? A <u>short</u> and <u>distinctive</u> statement in a <u>language</u> that <u>motivates</u> the buyer to take action.

_____

_____

_____

_____

_____

D. Ask for a 10 minute meeting and offer two alternative dates and times.

_____

_____

E. Ask for their contact information and send a confirmation email.

_____

_____

Ask Questions

Within the first five minutes you must explain...

A. What business are you in?

_____

_____

B. What is your Value Proposition Statement? A <u>short</u> and <u>distinctive</u> statement in a <u>language</u> that <u>motivates</u> the buyer to take action

_____

_____

C. Who are your customers?

_____

_____

D. Why are you there?(Purpose)

_____

_____

E. Set the agenda (Process)

_____

_____

<u>**You need to determine**</u>

F. Maximum three situations or factual questions you need to know that you cannot obtain through the study process
    1.
    2.
    3.

G. Maximum four confirmation questions to demonstrate your professional preparation.
    1.
    2.
    3.
    4.

H. What four potential internal pressure questions might you ask?
    1.
    2.
    3.
    4.

I. What four potential external pressure questions might you ask?
    1.
    2.
    3.
    4.

J. What are their top three organizational or division goals?
    1.
    2.
    3.

Three Areas of Focus when Questioning the Customer

There are three types of questions, some of which you will use sparingly, others you'll use throughout your conversation; however, there will be times you go from one type of question to the next during the questioning process.

✓ External pressures – These questions are about gathering information that you cannot obtain through other sources such as the Internet. You may need to ask questions about customers, suppliers, competition, regulatory issues, and globalization.

✓ Internal pressures – These questions are more specific to the buyer's processes and are designed to uncover problems, concerns, or dissatisfaction within the company or a department. These questions are designed to probe and penetrate beneath the surface in an effort to uncover operational and financial areas of concern. These can be profits, operations, employees, processes, productivity, and company culture.

✓ Goals or Objectives – Goal and objective questions move you beyond the find, grow, and measure customer dissatisfaction.

APPENDIX 4
– Learn and Expose Questions

Learn Questions

A. What do you need to learn before you move to the expose portion of the S.A.L.E.S. Formula™?

_____

_____

Expose Questions

    B. What expose questions might you ask?
        1.
        2.
        3.
        4.
        5.

Solution Questions

    C. What two solution questions might you ask?
        1.
        2.

    D. Have they confirmed the benefit a solution would provide?
        Yes or No

APPENDIX 5
— *Solve*

Presentation Preparation

    A. Who else needs to be at this presentation?

_____

_____

    B. Where will this presentation takes place?

_____

_____

    C. Have you reviewed the presentation room? Yes or No

_____

_____

    D. Have you confirmed a presentation time?

_____

_____

    E. Have you confirmed the time and all those attending by e-mail?

_____

_____

F. Has the following been addressed in your presentation?

You are positioned appropriately for my preparation, stories.

- Who you are
- WIIFT (what's in it for them)
- Agenda (what you'll discuss)
- Opening statement
- Personality types (Have you considered this?)
- Address possible objections
- 10-20-30
- Prepared a general proposal including
  1. Cover page
  2. Executive Summary
  3. Situation Analysis
  4. Goals and Objectives
  5. Challenge and Implications
  6. Recommended Solutions
  7. Appendix

- Made it easy for them to say yes
- Asked for the business!

RECOMMENDED READING

There are many great books on sales, marketing, presenting, leadership, and self- improvement. Most are available through your local bookstore in paperback, digital, and audio. Whatever your preference, I suggest any of the following.

Self Improvement

- Maximum Achievement: Strategies and Skills That Will Unlock Your Hidden Powers to Succeed – Brian Tracy
- Awaken the Giant – Anthony Robbins
- Unlimited Power – Anthony Robins
- Think & Grow Rich – Napoleon Hill
- The Master Key System – Charles Haanel

Business Books

- Before You Quit Your Job – Robert Kiyosaki and Sharon Lechter
- The E Myth – Michael Gerber
- The Mirror Test: Is Your Business Really Breathing? – Jeffery Hayzlett
- Pour Your Heart Into It: How Starbucks Built a Company Once Cup at a Time – Howard Schultz
- The New Secret of CEOs: Two Hundred Global Chief Executives on Leading – Steve Tappin, Andrew Cave
- Be Different or Be Dead, Your Business Survival Guide – Roy Osing
- Blue Ocean Strategy: How to Create Uncontested Market Space and Make Competition Irrelevant – W. Chan Kim, Renee Mauborgne

Marketing

- Trump University Marketing 101: How to Use the Most Powerful Ideas in Marketing to Get More Customers – Don Sexton
- Marketing 3.0: From Products to Customers to the Human Spirit – Philip Kotler, Hermawan Kartajaya, Iwan Setiawan

Selling

- Selling You! A Practical Guide to Achieving the Most by Becoming Your Best – Napoleon Hill
- Selling to Big Companies – Jill Konrath
- Selling Change – Brett Clay
- Sales 2.0: Improve Business Results Using Innovative Sales Practices and Technology – Anneke Seley, Brent Holloway
- Selling to Vito (The Very Important Top Officer) – Anthony Parenello
- Little Red book of Selling – Jeffrey Gitomer
- Selling to the C-Suite – Nicholas A. C. Read and Dr. Stephen J. Bistritz
- Selling to Zebra – Jeff Koser and Chad Koser
- A Seat at the Table: How Top Salespeople Connect and Drive Decisions at the Executive Level – Marc Miller
- Sales Techniques – Bill Brooks
- 10 Steps to Sales Success: The Proven System That Can Shorten the Selling Cycle, Double Your Close Ratio – Tim Breithaupt

Networking

- Social Boom! – Jeffrey Gitomer
- The Zen of Social Media Marketing – Shama Kabani and Chris Brogan
- Sociable! How Social Media is Turning Sales and Marketing Upside Down – Shane Gibson and Stephen Jagger
- 30 minute Social Media Marketing: Step-by-step Techniques to Spread the Word About Your Business – Susan M. Gunelius

- Twitter Power: How to Dominate Your Market One Tweet at a Time – Joel Comm

Presentations

- Presentation Zen: Simple Ideas on Presentation Design and Delivery – Garr Reynolds
- Slide:ology: The Art and Science of Creating Great Presentations – Nancy Duarte
- Real Leaders Don't Do Powerpoint: How to Sell Yourself and Your Ideas – Christopher Witt and Dale Fetherling

Sales Websites

- Aceofsales.com
- Eyesonsales.com
- Salesgravy.com
- Sellingpower.com
- Candogo.com
- Smei.org
- Insightfulselling.com
- Insightfulexecutive.com

NOTES:

1. Charles W. Hoyt, Scientific Sales Management [New Haven, CT; George W. Woolson & Co., 1913]
2. Ingram, Laforge, Avila, Schwepker Jr, Williams. Sixth Edition, Sales Management: Analysis and Decision Making.
3. Anneke Seley and Brent Holloway, Sales 2.0: Improve Business Results Using Innovative Sales Practices and Technology
4. Jeff Immelt, CEO, General Electric. From Customer Intimacy by Fred Wiersema
5. Forward by Neil Rackham of Selling is Dead, 2005
6. Forward by Neil Rackham of Selling is Dead, 2005
7. Tim Breithaupt, 10 Steps to Sales Success, 1999. Page 156
8. Mark Miller, Selling is Dead, 2005. Page 144
9. http://www.businessdictionary.com
10. Steve Tappin and Andrew Cave, The Secrets of CEOs: 150 Global Chief Executives Lift the Lid on Business, Life and Leadership. 2008
11. Steve Tappin and Andrew Cave, The Secrets of CEOs: 150 Global Chief Executives Lift the Lid on Business, Life and Leadership. 2008
12. Steve Tappin and Andrew Cave, The Secrets of CEOs: 150 Global Chief Executives Lift the Lid on Business, Life and Leadership. 2008
13. Philip Kotler, Marketing Insights from A to Z: 80 Concepts Every Manager Needs to Know
14. Mark Miller, Selling is Dead, 2005
15. http://www.businessdictionary.com
16. http://www.businessdictionary.com
17. http://www.businessdictionary.com
18. http://www.businessdictionary.com
19. http://www.businessdictionary.com

20. http://www.businessdictionary.com
21. http://www.businessdictionary.com
22. http://www.businessdictionary.com
23. http://www.businessdictionary.com
24. http://www.businessdictionary.com
25. http://www.businessdictionary.com
26. Steve Tappin and Andrew Cave, The Secrets of CEOs: 150 Global Chief Executives Lift the Lid on Business, Life and Leadership. 2008
27. Spectrum Sales Training , statistic, 10 Steps to Selling, 1999
28. Diane Bone, The Business of Listening: a Practical Guide to Effective Listening. 1988. Page 5
29. Brian Tracy, Advanced Selling Strategies
30. Val & Jeff Gee, Open-Question Selling: Unlock Your Customer's Needs to Close the Sale…by Knowing What to Ask and When to Ask It
31. Quote from Dr Cialdini
32. Snyder, Kearns. Escaping the Price Driven sale: How World Class Sellers Create Extraordinary Profit. Page 174
33. Sue Knight, NLP at Work: The Essence of Excellence, Second Edition,
34. Neil Rackham, SPIN Selling, 1988

About the Author

Adon Rigg began his sales career at age 18 with no money, no home, and a grade 8 education. With a passion for the sales process, he has worked his way from selling vacuums door-to-door to providing sales, training, and public speaking services for Fortune 500 organizations. Always eager to embrace lifelong learning, Adon is a graduate of the University of British Columbia Sales and Marketing program, and has received the CME and CSE designations for distinction in Sales and Marketing management. He has represented the province of British Columbia at the Canadian Association of Public Speakers Rising Stars Contest, and his S.A.L.E.S. Formula™ Program has been incorporated into the Business Certification Program at the University of the Fraser Valley in British Columbia, Canada.

Adon's philosophy is that no matter who you're selling to, from the CEO to the entry-level purchaser, all buyers are either directly or indirectly responsible for their Company's bottom line. He believes that the key to success is to learn how not to simply sell product, but to create value by impacting bottom-line results. To assist in the learning process, Adon has created The S.A.L.E.S Formula™, an acronym-based selling methodology that outlines the steps involved in his new Sales Process.

Adon's mission statement is "To help salespeople and entrepreneurs simplify their selling process by creating customer value using the S.A.L.E.S. Formula™."

Adon is CEO of Insightful Selling Solutions and author of the upcoming book "Insightful Selling: How to use the S.A.L.E.S Formula™ to differentiate yourself and create customer value".
You can contact Adon:

> By email: adon@insightfulselling.com
> On Facebook: www.facebook.com/adonrigg
> On Twitter: www.twitter.com/adonrigg
> On Linkedin: www.linkedin.com/in/adonrigg

> Free Resources at www.insightfulexecutive.com

> To learn more about Adon Rigg visit: www.insightfulselling.com

INDEX

Made in the USA
Charleston, SC
11 January 2012